SCOTLAND'S SCENIC HERITAGE

COUNTRYSIDE COMMISSION
FOR SCOTLAND

ISBN 0 902226 42 8

PREFACE

by Dr. Jean Balfour, Chairman,
Countryside Commission for Scotland.

In the Commission's report, *A Park System for Scotland,* we devoted a chapter to the question of landscape conservation and said that we had set in hand a review of areas of unsurpassed attractiveness which must be conserved as part of our national heritage. In this further report we set out the results of this review which has now been submitted to the Secretary of State.

We are confident that all of the 40 areas which we have selected will find general acceptance as being of outstanding scenic beauty. There will be many further areas which informed readers may consider could also have been included. We believe that many such areas will be of interest, particularly to local communities. In such cases it will be important for these areas to be identified and conserved by the local authorities concerned.

In the course of our review we have gathered a considerable amount of relevant information which we would be glad to make available to planning authorities, and which we hope will prove useful in the preparation of regional and local plans. The Commission looks forward to close consultation about ways in which policies might be developed for the conservation of this aspect of Scotland's national heritage.

Jean Balfour
April 1978

FOREWORD

by the Lord Kirkhill,
Minister of State for Scotland.

The scenery of Scotland is renowned throughout the world, and one aspect of being Minister of State at the Scottish Office with responsibility for planning and conservation which gives me great satisfaction is the opportunity to develop policies for the way in which we use our fine countryside. Planning is about choice — choice as to the way in which we use our resources, whether to exploit assets or to conserve them, whether to use them wisely or unwisely. When our successors look at how we have faced up to our responsibilities to conserve our national heritage, it is the way in which we have gone about making these choices by which we shall be judged.

Surprisingly there has been up to now no overall assessment of Scottish scenery and I have therefore encouraged the Countryside Commission for Scotland to look at this question and to produce advice which will help all of us in the planning process in central government and in planning authorities throughout the country. This the Commission have now done and the outcome of their work is set out in this report.

Scenic quality is essentially an aesthetic matter which does not readily lend itself to objective assessment. Nevertheless, the Commission have managed to introduce a degree of objectivity into the way in which they have tackled this job and I am sure that the report will be referred to as the basic working document for all those interested in this subject for many years to come.

This assessment offers a basis for the development of a new framework for landscape conservation. While the document will no doubt be referred to widely and for many purposes, its main aim is to focus the attention of planning authorities on areas of particular scenic distinction which, from the national standpoint, are of outstanding importance. This should be of help in the preparation of structure and local plans and I would expect to see the work of the Commission on scenic areas taken into account in the policies proposed by authorities for these areas.

In their introduction the Commission discuss their ideas about management agreements which were first put forward in the report "A Park System for Scotland." The further proposals which the Commission make on this will obviously need to be the subject of consultation between the Government, the Commission, and local authorities. At the outset I said planning was about choice. This report provides a basis for some of these choices. It therefore gives me great pleasure to commend this work to planning authorities and to the much wider readership which is also interested in the Scottish countryside.

John Kirkhill

CONTENTS

Part I: **Conservation of the Scenic Heritage**

             Introduction 2

             Existing Designations and Methods of Assessment 3

             National Scenic Areas 7

             Other Scenic Areas 10

             Safeguarding Scenic Areas 10

Part II: **The National Scenic Areas**

             Introduction and List of Areas 15

             Maps and Descriptions 16-97

    Bibliography 99

    Distribution map .... end paper

PART I CONSERVATION OF THE SCENIC AREAS

INTRODUCTION

1.1 The countryside is one of Scotland's basic assets and has to serve a wide variety of purposes. First and foremost, the land may be seen as the fundamental resource of the farming and forestry industries and it is subject to change on account of the development of new techniques in these industries and on account of changing land-use between one and the other. The countryside also has to accommodate demands for land for new housing and manufacturing industry around towns and cities and for major road improvements. In recent times quite major developments have taken place or have been proposed in areas discrete from established settlements, some of these areas being fairly remote from the main concentrations of population and previously thought of as being comparatively secure from major changes in land use. In some parts of the countryside the scenery is significantly influenced by management for sporting purposes, particularly for deer and grouse. The scenic attractiveness of the countryside is also important to the tourist industry, which has become increasingly significant in terms of balance of payments and as a provider of employment in Scotland. Even more importantly, however, the countryside should also be seen as a place of great beauty and attractiveness in its own right to be enjoyed by the people who live and work in Scotland.

1.2 It is the nation's responsibility to watch over and cherish this asset and to pass it on to future generations in a way which will show that proper care and concern have been taken to accommodate necessary new developments and to retain the natural attractiveness and amenity which the community has inherited from its predecessors. Outline proposals about how this might be achieved were set out in the Commission's report *A Park System for Scotland* which was submitted to the Secretary of State in 1974 and published in January 1975. These outline proposals were generally accepted by government in March 1976 after wide consultation with local authorities and other interests.

1.3 In the report *A Park System for Scotland* the Commission considered carefully the question of developing national parks in Scotland on the lines adopted in many other countries throughout the world and concluded that, for a variety of reasons relating to the form of central and local government organisation and of land-ownership and management, national parks would require a radical new approach to conservation in Scotland. We concluded that the same objectives of improving opportunities for the enjoyment of the countryside, whilst conserving its recreational and scenic attributes, could be achieved in other ways. The Commission's proposals were then divided into two broad parts. The first relates to the making of recreational provisions where these are required and the second to the development of policies and procedures for the conservation of those areas of countryside of unsurpassed attractiveness which are part of the national heritage, but which for the most part do not need significant recreational provisions to be made in them. The present report takes up the question of conservation of areas of outstanding scenic interest and sets out the results of a major review which the Commission has carried out to identify those parts of Scotland which require this particular care and attention.

1.4   We have not found or been able to develop any completely objective system capable of satisfactorily comprehending the selection of scenery in a way which would satisfy the essentially aesthetic aspects of the appreciation of natural beauty and amenity. The review has therefore been carried out on a systematic but subjective basis. In the next and succeeding sections of this report we describe how we have gone about the selection of areas which we consider to be of national significance and then we list the areas which we have so identified. We believe that this identification of outstanding scenic areas is a realistic and informed assessment which provides a useful basis for a review of existing landscape policies. This will enable the development of a new framework for landscape conservation, as forecast in the *National Planning Guidelines for Large Industrial Sites and Rural Conservation,* issued by the Scottish Development Department in May 1977.

1.5   In the meantime, the Commission has decided to publish the results of its work as the basis for further discussion of this important subject. In particular the Commission looks forward to discussions with planning authorities throughout Scotland in whom is vested prime responsibility for the development of planning strategies and development control policies for the countryside.

EXISTING DESIGNATIONS AND THE METHOD OF ASSESSMENT

2.1   The existing arrangements under the Planning Acts to secure the conservation of scenic interest fall into two categories. First, there is provision for national oversight in five areas which were identified in directions issued by the Secretary of State in 1948. These areas were those suggested for designation as national parks in Scotland in reports submitted by the Scottish National Parks Survey Committee (Cmnd 6631, HMSO 1945) and the Scottish National Parks Committee (Cmnd 7235, HMSO 1947). These directions were issued to secure a measure of added planning control in the context of a decision not to apply to Scotland the provisions of the National Parks and Access to the Countryside Act, 1949 other than those sections dealing with nature conservation. To safeguard the situation in what were felt then to be the most important scenic areas, the directions required the relevant local planning authorities to submit for scrutiny by the Secretary of State all applications for developments under the Planning Acts within the specified areas, and gave the Secretary of State an ability to call in for determination any which he considered warranted such action. The areas affected by these directions were:—

	Square miles
Loch Lomond/Trossachs	320
Glen Affric/Glen Cannich/Strathfarrar	260
Ben Nevis/Glen Coe/Blackmount	610
The Cairngorms	180
Loch Torridon/Loch Maree/Little Loch Broom	500

The second category of special planning provisions was the designation by planning authorities in their development plans of Areas of Great Landscape Value where the authorities themselves chose to operate special development control policies intended to conserve the particular scenic or landscape interest of the areas so designated.

2.2 In addition to the five National Park Direction Areas the Scottish National Park Survey Committee identified three reserve areas which were:—

	Square miles
Moidart/Morar/Knoydart	410
Glen Lyon/Ben Lawers/Schiehallion	140
St. Mary's Loch	180

As part of our background survey work for the preparation of the report *A Park System for Scotland* we prepared a series of descriptive essays on the five National Park Direction Areas, together with the Outer Hebrides, Knoydart, the Inner Isles and Galloway. It seemed to us sensible to begin our examination of the scenic resources of Scotland with these areas which had commended themselves to earlier workers in this field and then to go on to examine other areas which either suggested themselves to us in the course of the survey or were already covered by other conservation designations signifying a possible scenic interest.

2.3 In 1971, in an attempt to further the developments of an objective system of scenic assessment, the Commission published the study *A Planning Classification of Scottish Landscape Resources* (CCS Occasional Paper No. 1), prepared for us by Land Use Consultants. In an annex to that paper the consultants describe a method for landscape assessment. We tested this method and came to the conclusion that, although containing a good analytical approach to landscape, it attempts to combine objective analysis and subjective judgement in a way which does not produce satisfactory results nor leads, as intended, to evaluative comparisons of different landscape types. We have looked carefully at the work done by the late Professor Linton in relation to landscape assessment in Scotland and at other similar techniques that have been attempted in Europe and North America, but have found none that we have felt able to adopt for this review. Accordingly, as already indicated, we have adopted an approach to the identification of scenic resources which is based on the subjective judgement of assessors.

2.4 In summary, we have sought to identify scenery which best combines those features which are most frequently regarded as beautiful. On the whole this means that richly diverse landscapes which combine prominent landforms, coastline, sea and freshwater lochs, rivers, woodlands and moorlands with some admixture of cultivated land are generally the most prized. Not all of these features occur, however, in all the areas we have identified. Diversity of ground cover may be absent in some, but compensated for by especially spectacular landform or seascape. In Scotland, outstanding examples of such scenery are most frequently found north of or on the Highland Boundary Fault. We have recognised that many of the more managed landscapes to the south and east, in areas of intensive agricultural activity, are very beautiful but we have found it difficult to recognise many of these as being outstanding in a national or international sense. We have examined the Southern Uplands of Scotland most carefully, aware that the subtler landforms and more managed landscapes found there make comparison with Highland scenery difficult. We are aware that this is a kind of scenery not replicated elsewhere and one which is very pleasing to the eye attuned to it. We have therefore sought to identify those parts of it which, while not exhibiting the same diversity of form as Highland Scotland, nevertheless combine pleasing physiography with varied land-use to provide scenery of great charm and soft beauty.

2.5 In many of the areas we have identified, the pattern of settlement is a contributing feature. These areas do not include large towns, but crofting townships, ancient ecclesiastical settlements and the planned villages of the nineteenth century improvers often add to the scene. There are exceptions, usually small industrial towns or villages dependent upon a major industry, but where these occur, they have been set in the midst of such fine scenery that we have felt no useful purpose could be served by contriving to exclude the settlements from the identified areas. We consider that this approach, carried out with care and consistency, is a reasonable course to follow in a subject which we have not found amenable to measurement in scientific terms.

2.6 The method which we have adopted for carrying out the survey is as follows. First, desk appraisals of maps of the Scottish countryside at 1/50,000 scale were carried out to determine the likely extent and character of fine scenery. This work commenced with the five National Park Direction Areas then moved on to the other areas already referred to in paragraph 2.2 and subsequently to others which have commended themselves in the course of this survey, or which in the opinion of our surveyors from their extensive knowledge of the Scottish countryside were worthy of study. Although the method suggested by Land Use Consultants was not applied in full, its approach to the analysis of map information was used as the basis for examining topographical maps. Literary sources (see bibliography) were examined for opinions that had been expressed by others about the character of areas being considered. Planning documents produced by local authorities and by national agencies, such as the Nature Conservancy Council and the Forestry Commission, and by private bodies, such as the National Trust for Scotland, were also scrutinised for information on other designations such as Areas of Great Landscape Value, National Nature Reserves, Forest Parks and certain National Trust properties. With this basic appraisal of the likely extent of areas of fine scenery, the surveyors then made field inspections to form opinions as to the extent of landscape tracts which, for reasons of diversity of landform, vegetation and/or ground cover, or other outstanding visual characteristics, appeared to merit recognition as national assets.

2.7 We consider it to be an important aspect of this work that we have been able to use the same surveyors throughout, thus providing consistency of view to the whole exercise. Not only has the same team carried out all the field survey work, with never less than two officers undertaking field examination of any particular area, but they have reported their findings to a senior staff steering group which has remained unchanged throughout the exercise. The proposals produced in this way have, in turn, been subjected to scrutiny by the Commission which includes members with acknowledged expertise in the fields of assessment of scenic quality and rural land use.

2.8 We have deliberately not analysed scenery in terms of its geology, geomorphology, pedology, climate, natural history or cultural history. This is not because we think these things are unimportant in their influence on the scene, but because we believe that enjoyment of fine scenery is based on a perception of the whole which does not depend on more formal kinds of analysis. In particular, a conscious effort has been made not to let individual specialisations influence choice: nor has an attempt been made to select scenery on a representative basis of all the different types of landscape which occur in Scotland. We hope that it will be recognised that many attractive areas have had to be omitted in the process of identifying and selecting only that which we consider to be the very best.

NATIONAL SCENIC AREAS

3.1 Using the procedure and methods just described, we have identified 40 areas which we consider to be of national scenic significance and which, in the terms used in Chapter 6 of our report *A Park System for Scotland,* we consider to be of unsurpassed attractiveness which must be conserved as part of our national heritage. Certain of these areas are already under significant recreational pressure and will be proposed as Special Parks when the necessary legislation has been enacted. The bulk, however, are areas which, for the most part, are not under severe recreational or other specific pressures at present. In total, these amount to 12.7% or approximately one-eighth, of the land and inland water surface of Scotland. In our view this is not an unreasonably large proportion for a country so renowned for its scenic beauty.

3.2 The distribution of the 40 areas which have been identified is shown on the end papers and they are listed over. Descriptions and more detailed maps for each area are given later in this report.

REGIONAL DISTRIBUTION

Region and Area   **Hectares**
Areas marked thus * lie in more than one Region.

Shetland Islands
Shetland   Total   11,600

Orkney Islands
Hoy and West Mainland   Total   14,800

Highland Region
Kyle of Tongue   18,500
North-west Sutherland   20,500
Assynt-Coigach   90,200
Wester Ross   145,300
Trotternish   5,000
The Cuillin Hills   21,900
The Small Isles   15,500
Morar, Moidart and Ardnamurchan   13,500
Loch Shiel   13,400
Knoydart   39,500
Kintail   15,500
Glen Affric   19,300
Glen Strathfarrar   3,800
Dornoch Firth   7,500
Ben Nevis and Glen Coe*   79,600
The Cairngorm Mountains*   37,400
                                      Total   546,400

Western Isles
South Lewis, Harris and North Uist   109,600
St. Kilda   900
South Uist Machair   6,100
                                      Total   116,600

Grampian Region
The Cairngorm Mountains*   29,800
Deeside and Lochnagar*   32,200
                                      Total   62,000

Tayside Region
Ben Nevis and Glen Coe*   4,500
Deeside and Lochnagar*   7,800
Loch Tummel   9,200
Loch Rannoch and Glen Lyon*   47,100
River Tay (Dunkeld)   5,600
River Earn (Comrie to St. Fillans)   3,000
                                      Total   77,200

Strathclyde Region

Ben Nevis and Glen Coe*		17,500
Loch na Keal, Isle of Mull		12,700
Lynn of Lorn		4,800
Scarba, Lunga and the Garvellachs		1,900
Jura		21,800
Knapdale		19,800
Kyles of Bute		4,400
North Arran		23,800
Loch Lomond*		16,200
	Total	122,900

Central Region

Loch Rannoch and Glen Lyon*		1,300
Loch Lomond*		11,200
The Trossachs		4,600
	Total	17,100

Fife Region   Nil

Lothian Region   Nil

Borders Region

Upper Tweeddale		10,500
Eildon and Leaderfoot		3,600
	Total	14,100

Dumfries and Galloway Region

Nith Estuary		9,300
East Stewartry Coast		4,500
Fleet Valley		5,300
	Total	19,100

Region or Islands Area	Scenic Areas (Hectares approx)	% Scottish Land Surface (approx)
Shetland	11,600	0.15
Orkney	14,800	0.19
Highland	546,400	6.93
Western Isles	116,600	1.48
Grampian	62,000	0.79
Tayside	77,200	0.98
Strathclyde	122,900	1.56
Central	17,100	0.22
Fife	—	0.00
Lothian	—	0.00
Borders	14,100	0.18
Dumfries and Galloway	19,100	0.24
Scotland	1,001,800	12.72%

100% = 7,877,500 ha

9

OTHER SCENIC AREAS

4.1 The corollary to selecting only the very best scenic areas for particular care and attention as part of the national heritage is an inference that the remaining areas of countryside are of less importance and there may be disappointment that some places widely acknowledged to be of considerable scenic attractiveness have not been included in the list set out in paragraph 3.2. However, we have given a great deal of thought to many parts of the countryside which do not appear in this final list and we hope that it will be understood that these areas, while of undoubted scenic merit, do not in our view match up to the high standards which we have set for the areas chosen. This does not mean that we do not consider them also to be of importance since many of these areas will be significant in regional terms. We believe that they also require conservation strategies and development control procedures which recognise this significance. The work which we have done in selecting areas of outstanding national interest has given us an opportunity to look widely at many such areas in Scotland and the information which we have obtained will, of course, be available to local authorities who may wish to consider areas for specific recognition in structure and local plans because of their scenic merit in regional terms.

4.2 There are also a number of places which are quite outstanding in themselves, but which are different in character and scale from the areas in our national list by virtue of their limited extent and uniformity or their singular nature. Many of these are already Conservation Areas in terms of the Town and Country Amenities Act, 1974 or would be suitable for recognition as such. We hope that policy statements prepared by Regional Councils on landscape conservation will take these smaller areas into account as well as the wider areas selected as being of national or of regional significance.

SAFEGUARDING SCENIC AREAS

5.1 So far in this report our prime concern has been with the selection of areas of outstanding national scenic significance. The identification of these areas is an important first step towards their conservation and appropriate development, but it is no more than a first step. There must now follow positive action for their protection and development in ways which take full account of their national or local significance. The ways in which this might be achieved are manifold, but we see them in two broad categories, on the one hand relating to the planning process and on the other to land management.

5.2 In regard to the planning process we have had preliminary discussions with the Scottish Office and it is our understanding that the Secretary of State has it in mind to institute new planning procedures to safeguard the nation's scenic heritage. These measures were foreshadowed in the *National Planning Guidelines* issued in May 1977 and the Commission suggests that they should include, first, an interim policy requiring the notification of certain classes of planning application within areas of national scenic significance and, second, longer term proposals for the preparation of appropriate planning strategies and development control policies. Various ways exist in the Planning Acts and in the Countryside (Scotland) Act 1967 for setting up appropriate arrangements for this purpose and we propose to have further discussions with the Scottish Office about the particular methods to be employed.

5.3 Responsibility for the preparation of planning strategies and development control policies is, however, a matter for planning authorities in the first instance and it is on these authorities that the main burden of conserving the nation's scenic heritage rests. We are confident that planning authorities will accept this responsibility willingly and with due regard to the national interest. We look forward to assisting them with advice based upon our broader interest in the whole of the countryside, extending as it does to over 98% of the land and inland water area of Scotland. However, under our existing arrangements for planning, the final responsibility for conserving that which is nationally important must lie with the Secretary of State as the ultimate authority and we think it is essential that some procedure is maintained to ensure that developments in areas of national scenic interest which do not comply with approved development plans should be referred to him before final decisions are taken.

5.4 The second category of conservation measures relates to land management. Whilst the basic appearance of our countryside is determined by its geology and geomorphology and the effects of climate and light, there is no doubt that the scenic interest is often greatly influenced by the way in which we use the land, clothing it with a pattern of vegetation and enclosure to produce that which may be visually satisfying. Many of the changes which affect the appearance of the countryside are not influenced by the formal planning process, notably changes in agricultural practice itself and changes between agriculture and forestry. We believe that it is possible to influence such changes of land-use to accommodate the national scenic interest where necessary, while still meeting land management requirements, for instance by modifying the shape of new planting to safeguard outlooks from public vantage points or by modifying grazing pressures to increase natural regeneration of woodlands in particular situations.

5.5 Where land management is modified to secure the national interest and there is a resultant loss of some financial benefit to the owner or occupier, we believe there is a case for meeting at least part of that cost from Exchequer funds. Proposals for management agreements to meet this kind of situation were included in Chapter 6 of our report *A Park System for Scotland* and we reaffirm that we believe that these management agreements, analogous to nature reserve agreements and forestry dedication schemes, should be seen as an important element of our proposals for the conservation of scenic resources. Since we made this proposal for management agreements in our previous report, however, we have had the benefit of substantial public comment and we are now of the view that it would not be reasonable to expect the cost of conserving the national scenic interest to be met, even in part, by the ratepayers of local authorities rather than by the nation as a whole through the Exchequer. We have therefore proposed to Government that our original ideas should be modified so that management agreements within areas of national scenic interest should be made between land managers and the Commission representing the national interest. It would still be possible, however, for this mechanism to be made available to planning authorities in regard to any areas of regional landscape interest which they later seek to identify in their structure and local plans. Local authority expenditure in this regard should, of course, be eligible for the usual countryside grant at 75% in designated countryside, and to special park authorities at whatever higher rate may be agreed in respect of land falling within Special Parks under our park system proposals.

5.6 We believe that the Commission's broad terms of reference, particularly those concerning the conservation and enhancement of the natural beauty and amenity of the countryside, make it possible for us to prepare and put forward fundamental and comprehensive proposals in respect of the selection and protection of the national scenic heritage in a way and to an extent not feasible heretofore. We think that the matters set out in this report represent such a comprehensive approach which will result in the conservation of our scenic heritage, whilst at the same time accommodating change and development in response to changing circumstances. The Commission looks forward to the discussions which will flow from publication of this report and hopes that these will lead to the action for the positive conservation of that heritage which we think essential for the long-term wellbeing of Scotland.

PART II THE NATIONAL SCENIC AREAS

Part II contains details of the 40 areas referred to in paragraph 3.2 of the report. For each area there is a description and a map. The description in each case consists of three sections, the first describing the location and extent of the scenic area, the second describing the scenic characteristics of the area, and a third relating to some other national interests in the area. This third section is not exhaustive and has been based on information available to the Commission from its own records. Generally it attempts to record national nature conservation interests, Forestry Commission ownerships, National Trust ownerships, Department of Agriculture and Fisheries for Scotland ownerships, Department of the Environment ownerships and the existing National Park Direction Areas, all factors which may have significance for the conservation of scenery. The Commission recognises that there are many other factors not recorded which will also have a bearing on the conservation of scenery.

Shetland	17
Hoy and West Mainland	21
Kyle of Tongue	23
North-west Sutherland	25
Assynt — Coigach	27
Wester Ross	29
Trotternish	31
The Cuillin Hills	33
The Small Isles	35
Morar, Moidart and Ardnamurchan	37
Loch Shiel	39
Knoydart	41
Kintail	43
Glen Affric	45
Glen Farrar	47
Dornoch Firth	49
Ben Nevis and Glen Coe	51
The Cairngorm Mountains	53
South Lewis, Harris and North Uist	55
St. Kilda	57
South Uist Machair	59
Deeside and Lochnagar	61
Loch Tummel	63
Loch Rannoch and Glen Lyon	65
River Tay (Dunkeld)	67
River Earn (Comrie to St. Fillans)	69
Loch na Keal, Isle of Mull	71
Lynn of Lorn	73
Scarba, Lunga and the Garvellachs	75
Jura	77
Knapdale	79
Kyles of Bute	81
North Arran	83
Loch Lomond	85
The Trossachs	87
Upper Tweeddale	89
Eildon and Leaderfoot	91
Nith Estuary	93
East Stewartry Coast	95
Fleet Valley	97

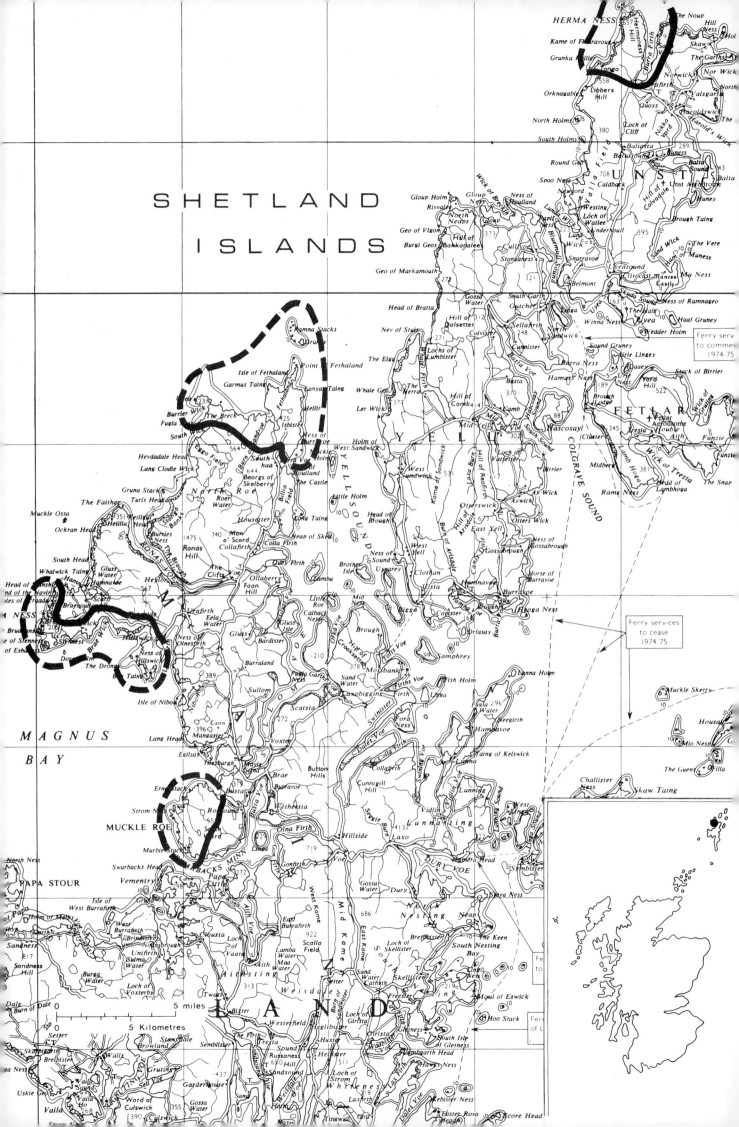

SHETLAND ISLANDS

HERMA NESS

The Noup
Hermaness Hill
Kame of Flouravoug
Skaw
Hill
Ness
Nor Wick
Norwick
The Garths
Grunka Hellier
Tonga
Burra Firth
Hol
Orknagable
Dobers Hill
Valsgarth
Quoys
Haroldswick
Harold's Wick The
North Holms
Loch of Cliff
Nikka Vord
Sand Wick
Loch of Cliff
380
The Vere
South Holms
U N S T
Ham of Muness
Round Geo
Caldback
Balta
Spoo Ness
Newgord
Colvadale
Unst Aerodrome
Balta Sound
Hill of Colvadale
Huney
Wick of Breckon
Ness of Houlland
Westing
Gloup Holm
Gloup Ness
Loch of Watlee
Brough Taing
Rivvalee
Underhoull
North Neaps
Gloup
373
Lund
Wick
395
Geo of Vigon
Hill of
Bankanalee
Sand Wick
Muness
Burgi Geos
Cullivoe
Belmont
Livocast
Muness Castle
Stonganess
Snarravoe
Uyeasound
Mu Ness
Geo of Markamouth
272
Skuda Sound
Ness of Ramnageo
Gossa Water
South Garth
Gutcher
Uyea Sound
321
Head of Bratta
Hill of Dalsetter
Sellafirth
Linga
163
Nev of Stuis
Colvister
North Sandwick
Winna Ness
Uyea
Haaf Gruney
Lochs of Lumbister
Cunnister
Basta Voe
Sound Gruney
Wedder Holm
The Elgs
248
Burra Ness
Urie Lingey
Whale Geo
377
The Herra
Basta
310
Hamars Ness
Uri
Nuss
Daaey
Stack of Birrier
Ler Wick
Hill of Camb
414
Camb
88
Brough Lodge
Yord Hill
522
Wick of Gruting
Holm of
West Sandwick
Mid Yell
Micla Voe
189
Tresta
FETLAR
West
Sandwick
Hascosay
Cluster
Fetlar Aerodrome
Houlland
Hill of Redfirth
Loch of Vatsetter
Birrier
Midbrek
Lamb Hoga
Funzie
The Castle
Bilia Field
302
Funzie
Little Holm
Hill of Arisdale
345
Head of Lambhoga
N O R T H
Long Taing
Otterswick
East Yell
Otters Wick
381
Rams Ness
The Snap
Roer Water
Housetter
Ay Wick
Colla Firth
Colla Firth
740
Neap of Skeo
Y E L L
S O U N D
Ness of Sound
Uyeasey
Gossaborough
Ness of Gossabrough
R O E
Brother Isle
Clothan
Hamnavoe
Horse of Burravoe
Quey Firth
Ollaberry
Lamba
Uista
Burravoe
The Clifts
Faan Hill
Little Roe
Mio Ness
Bigga
Brough
Hoga Ness
Heylor
567
Ufafirth
Eela Water
Calback Ness
Copister
Orfasay
Ness of Olnesfirth
Gluss Isle
Bardister
Brough
Gluss
Samphrey
Ness of Hillswick
Burraland
Hill of Crooksetter
378
Mossbank
Irish Holm
Lunna Holm
389
Sullom
Swinister
Fora Ness
Muckle Skerry
Isle of Nibon
Sand Water
Firths Voe
Linga
Fugla
Water
Neegirth
296
Scatsta
Voxter
272
Hambavoe
Housay
Cairn
396
Dales Voe
Challister Ness
Mio Ness
Lang Head
Mangaster
Skaw Taing
Egilsay
Colla Firth
Maing of Kelswick
The Guens
Filla
Islesburgh
Collafirth
Lunna
Muckle Roe Challister
Ern Stack
Busta
Button Hills
Lunning
Muckle Roe
Brae
Burravoe
Cunnigill Hill
West Lunna
Strom Ness
Roesound
Hill
Vidlin
South
Ward
Swinna Voe
Aldin Voe
Lunna Ness
Murbie Stacks
Olna Firth
Vidlin Voe
M A G N U S
Swarbacks Head
719
Hillside
Lunnasting
Lunning Sound
B A Y
North Ness
Vementry
Busta Voe
Dinna
Laxo
Mavis Head
Symbister
PAPA STOUR
Calva
Papa Little
Gonfirth
Voe
Dury Voe
Gossa Water
DURY VOE
Dury
Skaa Ness
Isle of West Burrafirth
Gruid
West Kame
Mid Kame
N O R T H
West Burrafirth
922
686
N E S T I N G
Neap
Horn of Moelly
West Burrafirth
Scalla Field
Brettabister
The Keen
Catholm
Brindister
Ousta
Lamba Water
Loch of Skellister
South Nesting Bay
Sandness
Hansbrough
Unifirth
Aith Water
Maa Water
Skellister
Sandness Hill
Sulma Water
Laxo Ness
Burga Water
Setter
Sand Water
Catfirth
Dale
A i t h s t i n g
313
Freester
Mool of Eswick
Burn of Dale
Twatt
W e i s d a l e
219
Setter
Westerfield
Loch of Girlsta
Hoo Stack
Browland
Skellberry
Girlsta
Gletness
South Isle of Gletness
Breibister
Sembister
Huxter
Walls
Gruting
Tresta
Spund
Russaness Hill
Lambgarth Head
650
437
Helister
511
Skaa Ness
Vaila Sound
Gardenhouse
Sandsound
Loch of Strom
511
Score Head
Vaila Ho
Gossa Water
W h i t e n e s s
318
Rebister Ness
355
390
Culswick
Tinwall
Dales Voe
Ward of Culswick
268
L A N D

Scale: 0 ___ 5 miles

0 ___ 5 Kilometres

Ferry service to commence 1974-75

Ferry services to cease 1974-75

SHETLAND ISLANDS AREA

11,600 HECTARES

SHETLAND

EXTENT OF AREA

A number of coastal landscapes in Shetland have been identified as of outstanding scenic interest. In seven separate small areas, they lie principally in the south-west and northern extremities of the archipelago and include Fair Isle, Foula, the western flank of Dunrossness and the Deeps, part of Muckle Roe, Esha Ness, Uyea Isle and Fethaland, and Herma Ness.

The margins of the Fair Isle and Foula areas are self-defining as the whole of each island is included. In the South West Mainland the eastern margin is defined by the summit ridge of Garths Ness and the Cleap, the Burn of Hillwell, the public road B9122 as far north as Bigton, the summit ridge of Ness of Ireland, and that of the Clift Hills as far north as the Trondra Causeway. Scalloway is excluded, and the summit ridges of the hills of Berry, Burwick, and Nesbister continue northward on the eastern limit of the area. At Wormadale the public road defines the eastern extent of the area as far north as Cova. From there the margin swings west through Hostaberg (197m) to include Russa Ness, Fora Ness, Sand Voe, Seil Voe, Roe Ness, Skelda Voe and the east flank of Skelda Ness, terminating at Spoot Hellier.

At Muckle Roe, that part of the island lying west of a line drawn through Ward Hill from Burki Taing to Stabaness is included.

At Esha Ness, the Ness of Hillswick and all the coast south of the public road B9078 from the north shore of Sand Wick to the junction with the side road to Caldersgeo is included. From that side road the coast northwards below the first inland summit ridge is included as far as Head of Stanshi.

At Fethaland the public roads from Burgo Taing to Greenfield on the northern side of the village of North Roe, and then the summits of Hill of Sandvoe, Saefti Hill, Heogel of the Moor and Fugla Ness define the southern limit, to the north of which all the peninsula, Ramna Stacks and Uyea Isle are also included in the scenic area.

At Herma Ness the area covered by the National Nature Reserve is included, together with Burra Firth as enclosed by the public road B9086 and the track northwards to Holey Kame, north of which the summits of Saxa Vord and the Noup define the eastern extent of the area.

DESCRIPTION

Scenic interest in Shetland is predominantly coastal. Fair Isle is a combination of green fields, moors and sandstone cliffs, all related to the coast. Remote from the mainland of Shetland, it has a great diversity of cliffs, geos, stacks, skerries, natural arches, isthmuses and small bayhead beaches. It is one of the foremost bird observatories in Europe. While it lacks great absolute relief, it has the distinctive features of Sheep Rock and the several eminences of its west coast which add further variety to the coastal scenery.

Foula, because of its greater height (418m), enjoys a more direct visual relationship to the mainland and boasts cliffs in the Kame rising to 366m. The striking form of the island contributes greatly to the coastal scenery of the South West Mainland. The coast of the island itself exhibits a diversity of natural features, including stacks, cliffs, skerries, caves and headlands.

Within the South West Mainland area, stretching from Fitful Head to the Deeps, there is a variety of contrasting landscapes ranging from cliffed coastline of open aspect in the south to fjord-like indentation in the voes of Weisdale and Whiteness. The larger islands of Burra and Trondra have distinctive settlement patterns, and the other numerous small islands and stacks lying in the bight known as the Deeps all combine to make a western oceanic seascape of strong character and atmosphere in which the constantly changing skies play an important part. The area is further diversified and enhanced by the softer features of St. Ninian's Isle with its fine tombolo and the adjacent enclosed and humanised landscape around the Loch of Spiggie.

At Muckle Roe a further significant element of Shetland scenery is found in the remarkable high red sandstone cliffs which make a significant contribution to the wider coastal scene of St. Magnus Bay of which they are the outstanding feature, together with the fine headlands, cliffs, skerries and stacks of Esha Ness.

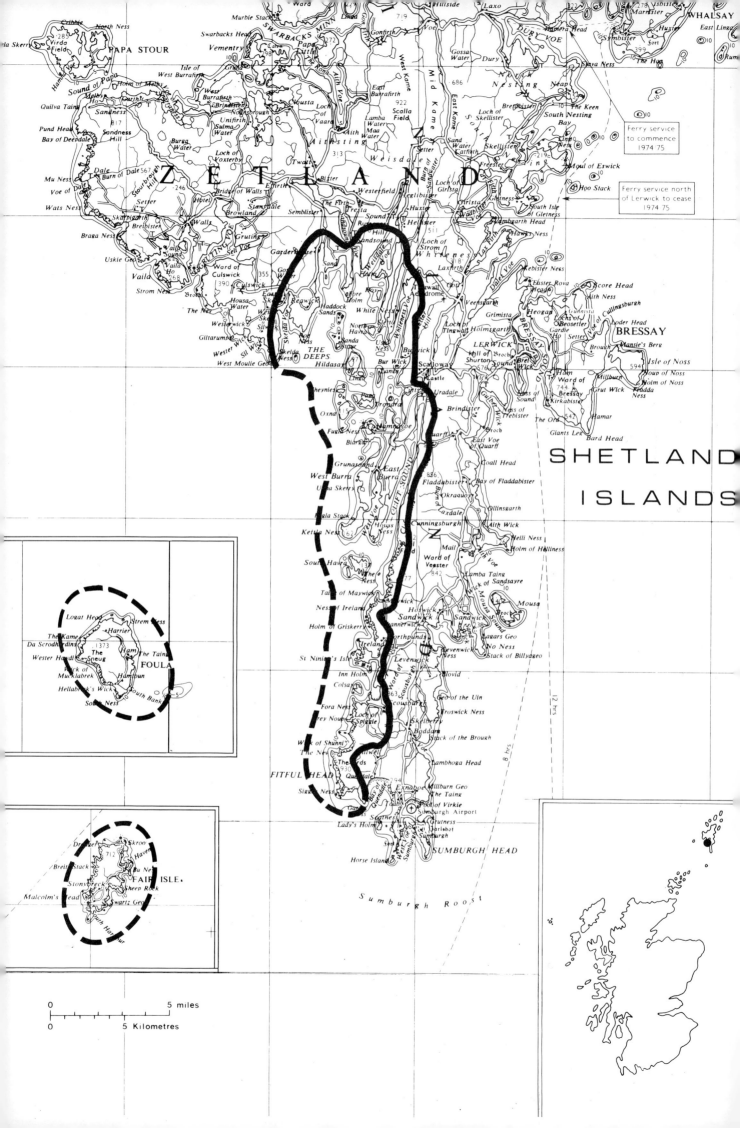

SHETLAND ISLANDS AREA

11,600 HECTARES

Further north, the northern extremities of the North Roe peninsula again exhibit a similar range of skerries, stacks, islets, geos, caves, headlands and natural arches, to which the complex geology lends further variety of colour and form between Fugla Ness, Uyea Isle, Fethaland and the Ramna Stacks, and the Ness of Burravoe. Hermaness and Burrafirth including Muckle Flugga and Out Stack, at the northern extremity of the British Isles, are of the same outstanding character.

OTHER NATIONAL INTERESTS

The area includes the National Nature Reserve at Hermaness and the RSPB reserve at Ramna Stacks. Fair Isle is a property of the National Trust for Scotland, and also a Site of Special Scientific Interest, as is Foula. In the Dunrossness area there are three Sites of Special Scientific Interest — at Whiteness, St. Ninian's Isle and Loch of Spiggie.

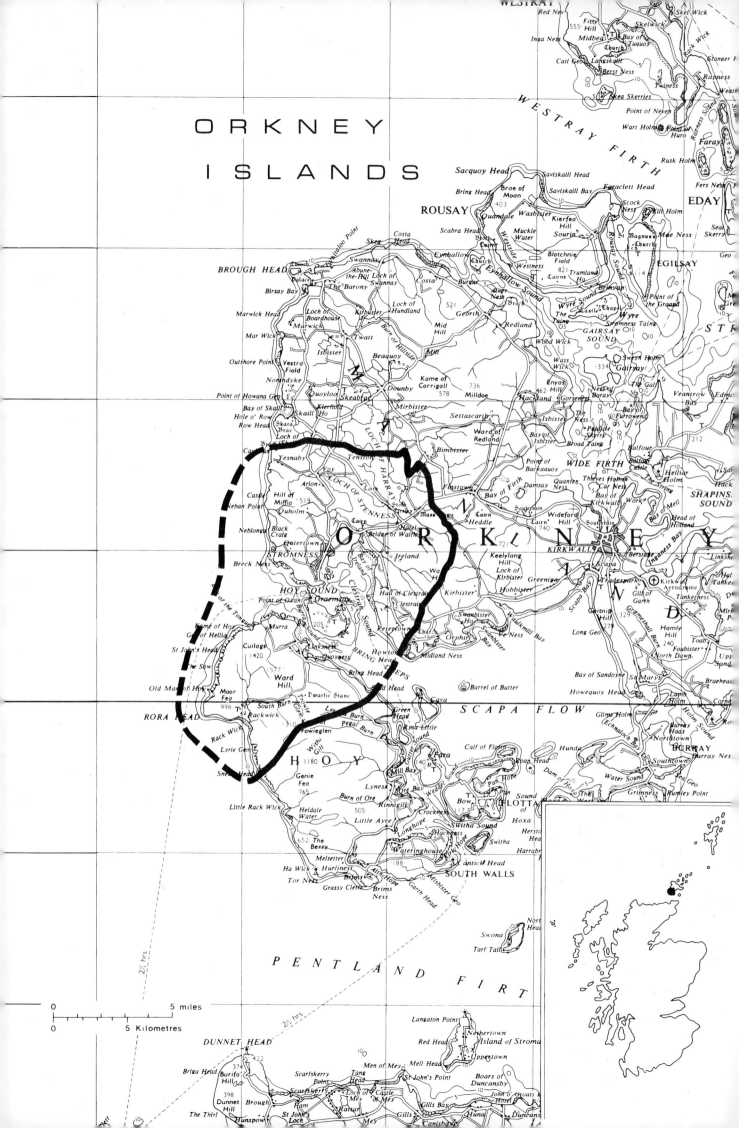

ORKNEY ISLANDS AREA **HOY AND WEST MAINLAND**

14,800 HECTARES

EXTENT OF AREA

The area includes the hills of North Hoy, Hoy Sound, Graemsay and part of the South West Mainland extending from Yesnaby to Ward Hill and enclosing the Loch of Stenness and the southern part of the Loch of Harray.

The seaward limits of the area extend from Bor Wick in the north, south past the cliffs of Yesnaby and Hoy to Sneuk Head. The Parish boundary of Hoy and Graemsay defines the southern limit which continues across the Bring Deeps to Houton Head. From there the eastern limits follow the summits of Hill of Midland, Hill of Dale, Gruf Hill, Ward Hill and South Rusky Hill to the public road at Nisthouse. The public road is followed northwards to its junction with the public road A965 which is followed westwards to the junction with the public road to Grimeston. This latter road is followed north as far as Netherbrough, where the narrows of Loch of Harray are crossed westwards to Ness of Tenston. From here a line due west skirting the north bank of the Loch of Clumly to Bor Wick identifies the northern extent of the area.

DESCRIPTION

The great ice-rounded eminences of the hills of North Hoy dominate the Orkney scene with a power that is scarcely in tune with their modest height (479 metres). Their bold shape, fine grouping, soaring cliffs and headlands, including the famous stack of the Old Man of Hoy, are almost as important to the Caithness scene as they are in that of Orkney. North Hoy has a particularly strong visual inter-relationship with the south-west mainland of Orkney, the pastoral character of which around the shores of the Loch of Stenness makes a good foil for the bold hills of Hoy. The basin of this loch is enclosed by low rolling hills of lush grassland, some arable land, scattered farm steadings and stone dykes with a noticeable lack of trees, giving a very open landscape, the character of which is enlivened by the abundant remains of ancient occupation. This landscape culminates in the west in cliffed headlands like a rampart against the sea, which breaks through at Hoy Sound in a tidal race of impressive swiftness. The stone-built settlement of Stromness rising steeply out of its harbour further enhances the character of the area.

OTHER NATIONAL INTERESTS

Many ancient monuments in Orkney are under the protection of the Department of the Environment. There are Sites of Special Scientific Interest at North Hoy, Ward Hill, Yesnaby, and the Lochs of Stenness and Harray. The Forestry Commission owns small parcels of land in North Hoy.

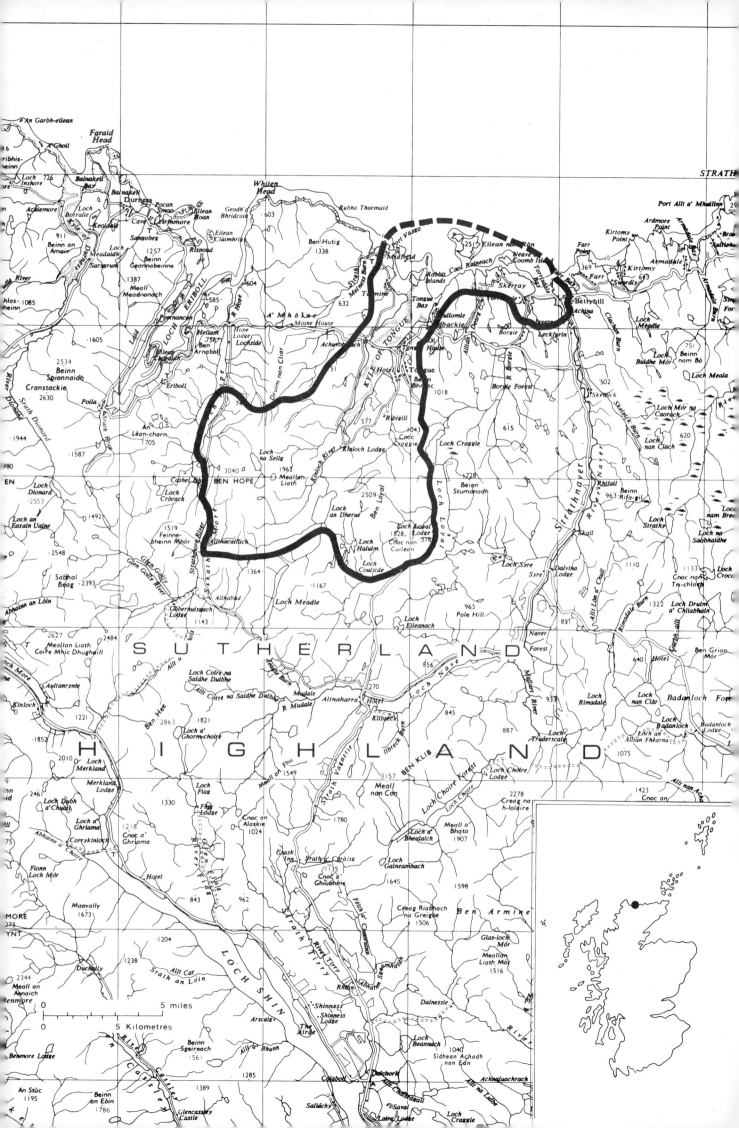

HIGHLAND REGION   KYLE OF TONGUE

18,500 HECTARES

EXTENT OF AREA

This area extends from the east shore of Torrisdale
Bay in the east, westwards along the coast of
Sutherland including Neave Island, Eilean nan Ron
and the Rabbit Islands to Port Vasgo in the west. The
western margin is defined by the watershed west of
Talmine, the ridge of Cnoc Lon nan Eildean, part of
the Moine Path, Creagan na Speireig, and the public
road to Dun Dornaigil Broch. The southern margin
runs from the broch eastwards via Carn Achaidh,
Creag Riabhach and Creag an Achaidh Mhoir to
Dherue, then on via Loch Haluim to skirt the
southern flank of Ben Loyal along Loch Coulside to
the public road at Inchkinloch. The eastern margin
follows this road (A836) northwards to a point one
mile south of Kirkboll (Tongue) and then follows the
summit ridge of a series of low hills including Ben
Tongue and Ben Blandy to follow the first inland
summit ridge around the coast to Torrisdale and
Invernaver. The estuary of the Naver west of the
public road (A836) is included with the western flank
of the headland of Creag Ruadh.

DESCRIPTION

Ben Hope (927m) and Ben Loyal (764m) are well
known as two of the finest mountains in the north of
Scotland. Their isolation in the landscape
emphasises on the one hand the massive asymmetric
cone of Ben Hope which dominates the northern
seaboard, and on the other the stately succession of
granite peaks of Ben Loyal which form a compelling
skyline at the head of the Kyle of Tongue. The Kyle of
Tongue itself exhibits a constantly changing
character with the ebb and flow of the tide, and the
varied woodlands and pattern of crofting settlements
along its shores add landscape diversity to the
scenic relationship it enjoys with the two bens. The
coastline at the mouth of the Kyle, with its islands,
cliffs and indented bays with sandy beaches and
crofting settlements, forms a visually related coastal
extension to the inner part of the Kyle. This character
extends in undiminished quality to the mouth of the
Naver in Torrisdale Bay.

OTHER NATIONAL INTERESTS

There is a National Nature Reserve at Invernaver,
and Sites of Special Scientific Interest at Ben Hope,
Ben Loyal, Eilean nan Ron and Aird Torrisdale. The
National Trust for Scotland has made Conservation
Agreements at Skelpick and Tongue Estates.

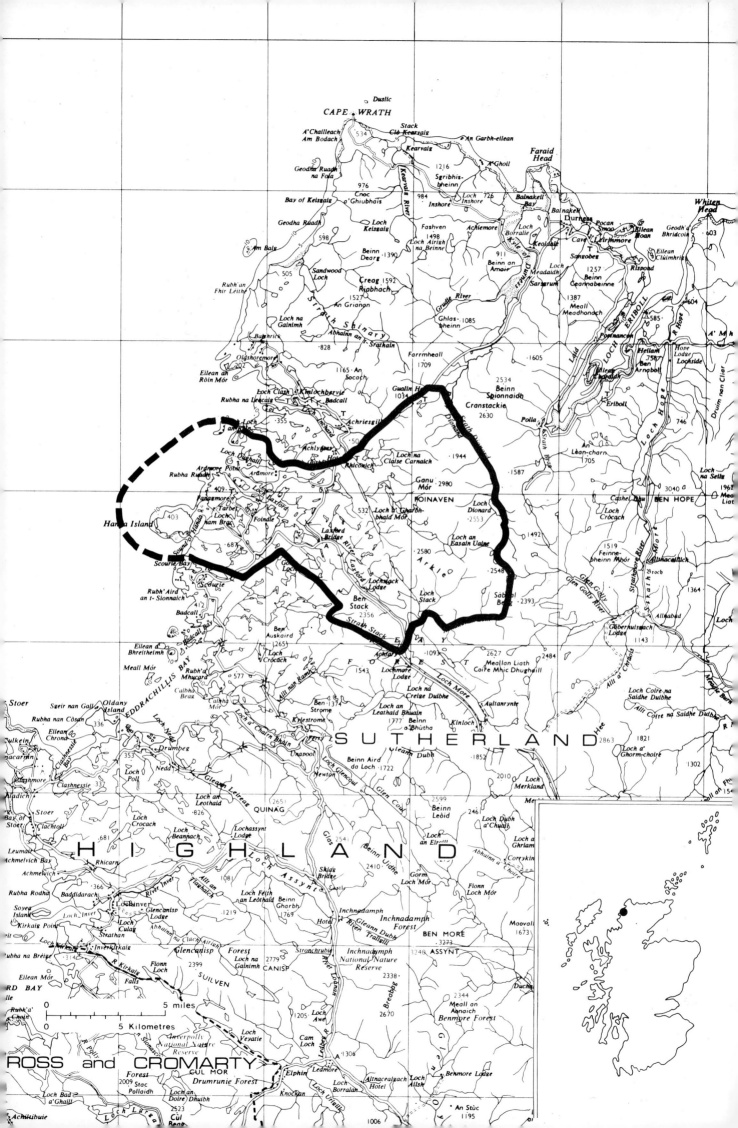

HIGHLAND REGION

NORTH-WEST SUTHERLAND

20,500 HECTARES

EXTENT OF AREA

This area includes the Foinaven-Arkle massif, the basin of the Laxford River to the head of Loch Stack and Handa Island. Its margin on the northern side is defined by the public road A838 from Gualin House to Rhiconich Bridge, and by the ridge of Ceathramh Garbh westwards to Loch an Roin and the Dubh Sgeirean. The western margin runs south over sea to include the island of Handa. The southern margin follows the first main ridge north of Scourie and south of Badnabay to Strathstack to follow the Allt Achfary. From Achfary the minor road to Lone, and the Abhainn an Loin identify the remainder of the southern margin. The eastern margin is identified by the River Dionard and the path which leaves the public road A838 near Gualin House to run up Strath Dionard.

DESCRIPTION

Foinaven, Arkle and Ben Stack are mountains of quartzite resting dramatically on Lewisian gneiss. Ben Stack (721m) is a shapely remnant cone, Arkle (787m) a whale-back, and Foinaven (909m) a long slab broken into separate summits. The summits and flanks of the latter two form a stark desert of white quartzite scree broken occasionally by lines of tiered crags. The knock and lochan topography of the gneiss landscape extending to the west forms a suitable foil for this varied trio, as hard and uncompromising as the mountains themselves. Loch Laxford is made up of the same bare rocky topography and is clearly related to the mountain core of the area. Its indented coast does not have the wooded inlets and bays that are found further south, but there are some sheltered beaches from which Handa Island with its towering sandstone cliffs and bird colonies can be seen.

OTHER NATIONAL INTERESTS

There is a National Nature Reserve at Gualin which lies within the Foinaven and Meall Horn and Loch Stack Site of Special Scientific Interest which covers the eastern part of the area. Other Sites of Special Scientific Interest are at Loch Laxford and Handa-Duartmore. Handa is also an RSPB reserve.

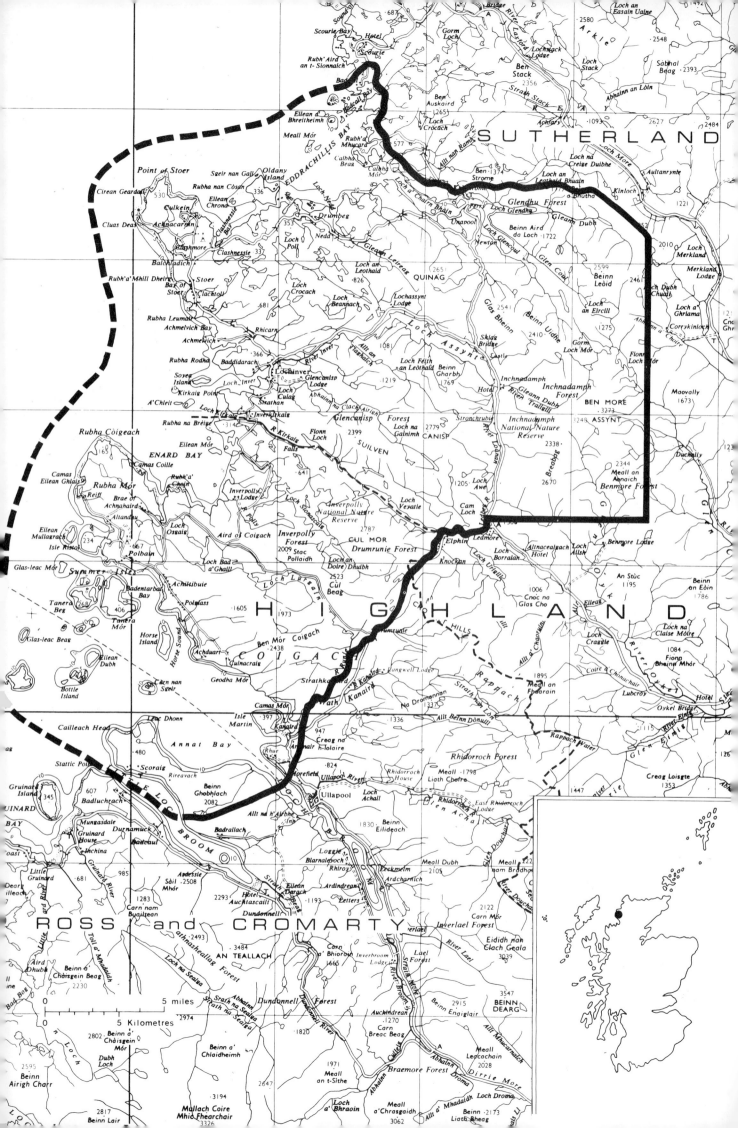

90,200 HECTARES

EXTENT OF AREA

The area extends from Eddrachillis Bay in the north to Loch Broom in the south and inland to Ben More Assynt. On the seaward margin the limits of the area run from Badcall in the north past the Point of Stoer and Rhu Coigach, around the Summer Isles in the south, to Loch Kanaird. The landward margin follows the River Runie in Strath Kanaird, and the public road A835 to Knockan, the River Knockan, the shore of Cam Loch, and the Ledbeg River to Ledbeg. Here an arbitrary limit corresponding to northing NC 13 has been followed east to grid reference NC 350130. The eastern inland margin corresponds to easting NC 35 extending as far north as NC 350320, whence the northern margin follows the ridge north of Glendhu and Kylestrome around the coast to Badcall.

DESCRIPTION

Assynt and Coigach present a landscape unparalleled in Britain. Steep hills with idiosyncratic profiles rise from hummocky surroundings in some of the most rugged and spectacular scenery in Scotland. The area contains seven well known mountains: Ben More Coigach, Stac Pollaidh, Cul Beag, Cul Mor, Suilven, Canisp and Quinag. They are famed for their strange spectacular shapes, which are thrown into relief, higher than their statistical height would indicate, by the comparatively uniform ground of moorland and loch out of which they rise. Some of them have knife-edged ridges of white quartz and grey scree slopes that contrast with the weathered red sandstone that forms the core of their structure. The contrasting lowlands are a jumble of morainic hillocks and pink-grey rock, interspersed with lochans and peaty hollows. Of Suilven, perhaps the most famous of these peaks, Frank Fraser Darling has written: 'There is only one Suilven and it is undoubtedly one of the most fantastic hills in Scotland. It rises 2,309ft (731m) out of a rough sea of gneiss . . . . probably the Dolomites would be the nearest place where such an extraordinary shape of hill could be seen.' The same might be said of Stac Pollaidh, and the other mountains are only different in form, but no less salient. To the east Ben More Assynt, lying east of the Moine Thrust, has a different character deriving from its different geological history. Its vaster bulk and wild, rugged grandeur form the backdrop to the drama of the peaks of Assynt and Coigach, mirrored as they are in tranquil weather in the lochs as Assynt, Veyatie, Sionascaig and Lurgainn.

The coast of the area is as diverse as the interior. Badcall Bay has a scatter of islands which catch the constantly changing western light. The long narrow sea loch of Loch a' Chairn Bhain and its tributaries Loch Glendhu and Loch Glencoul are surrounded by towering peaks and bare rugged hills. The Summer Isles off Achiltibuie form a broken seaboard to contrast with the solid mass of Ben More Coigach. A. Wainwright has written: 'The mountains, although sparsely distributed, are the dominant feature of the landscape, but in other respects too this area has great appeal. Around the seaboard is a richly diversified pattern of inlets and sandy bays, rivers and native woodlands; of hamlets and crofts that cling close to the narrow coastal fringe, because only there do land and sea provide a living.'

OTHER NATIONAL INTERESTS

There are National Nature Reserves at Inverpolly and Inchnadamph, and Sites of Special Scientific Interest at Knockan, Ben More Assynt and Breabag, Eilean na Gartaig, Loch Assynt Quarry, Loch Beannach, Loch Glencoul, the Ardvar Woodlands and Duartmore. The Forestry Commission owns land at Ledmore.

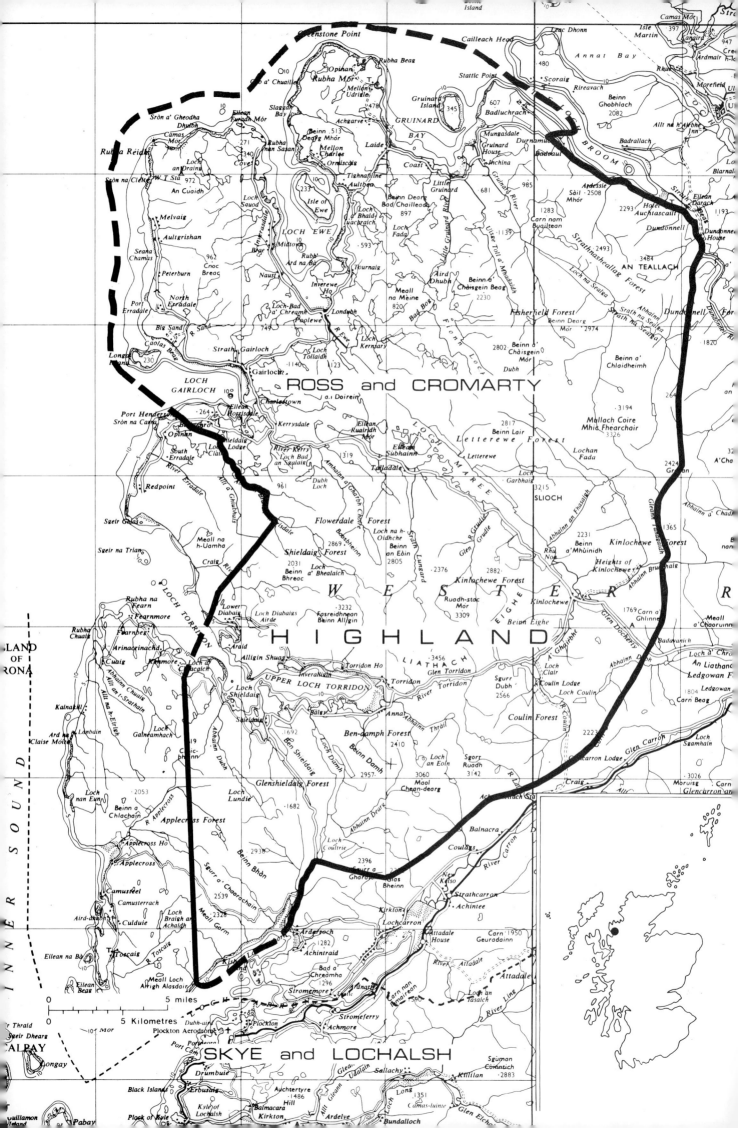

HIGHLAND REGION   WESTER ROSS

145,300 HECTARES

EXTENT OF AREA

The most extensive of the national scenic areas proposed, this area includes the Applecross Forest, the Ben Damph Forest, the Torridon Mountains, Loch Maree, the Letterewe Forest, the Fisherfield Forest, and the Strathnasheallag Forest. On the coast Gruinard Bay, Loch Ewe, Gairloch, Loch Torridon and part of Loch Kishorn are included. Part of the Red Point peninsula is excluded. The seaward margin runs from Sron na Faire Moire on the east shore of Gruinard Bay, west about Greenstone Point and Rubha Reidh to turn south as far as Loch Gairloch. Here the limits strike land east of Port Henderson to Loch Braigh Horrisdale and follow the burn to Loch Gaineamhach. From that loch an arbitrary margin running south-westwards to Loch a Cheacaich near Kenmore on the Applecross peninsula has been chosen, and from Kenmore, a line due south to Airighdrishaig represents the western landward margin. From Loch Kishorn the eastern margin has been identified with the public road A869 to Loch an Loin, whence it runs east to the summit of Glas Bheinn above Strathcarron and north east to Fuar Tholl, Cam Breac and Cam na Garbh Lice above Glen Docherty. From there the eastern margin skirts the Fisherfield Forest via the summits of Groban and Creag Rainich to the public road A832 at Corrie Hallie, Dundonnell. The public road is followed as far as the ridge of Druimnan Fuath, above Gruinard Bay, which declines into the sea at Sron na Faire Moire.

DESCRIPTION

The area combines six of the great mountain groups of Scotland. The names of the outstanding individual peaks and their profiles are perhaps better known than the slopes of the mountains themselves, and the descriptive literature is full of hyperbole, at which few beholders of the scene would demur. To traverse the area from the beetling crags and precipitous corries of the Applecross Forest to the jagged teeth of An Teallach is to experience a sustained crescendo of mountain scenery which could leave no spectator unmoved. Murray has described Liathach in the Torridon Group as 'the most soaring mountain in the North,' and many writers concur with his opinion that An Teallach 'is one of the half dozen most splendid mountains in Scotland,' and that 'its eastern corrie, Toll an Lochain, is one of the greatest sights in Scotland.' It would be superflous to describe the individual qualities of all the intervening mountains. For most people their names will suffice to conjure up the splendour of the scene: Ben Damph, Beinn Eighe, Beinn Alligin, Slioch, A' Mhaighdean, Mullach Coire Mhic Fhearchair, Bein Lair, Beinn Dearg Mhor. The area is frequently described as the last great wilderness of Scotland, but contains much that is of a serene and gentler beauty than the rugged splendour of mountain fastnesses.

Loch Maree has been described as 'one of the two most excellent of Scotland's big inland waters' (Murray) and 'the embodiment of what is called Highland Grandeur' (Weir). Of Loch Torridon, Wainwright writes: 'Without the loch, Torridon would be a fearful place, but with it, there is not a grander prospect to be found in Scotland.' Many other water bodies, notably Loch Shieldaig, Loch Damh, Loch Clair, the Fionn-Fada lochs, Loch-na-Sealga and Loch Tournaig contribute variety of character to the scene. With the exception of the Fionn-Fada group these lochs have in varying degrees shores which between rocky headlands are frequently wooded with semi-natural woodlands of oak, birch and Scots pine, which together with moorland and scrub soften the lower lying parts of the area to make a gentle foil for the starker mountains.

Around the coast Gruinard Bay, Loch Ewe and Loch Gairloch exhibit a pleasing mixture of beaches, islands, headlands, inlets, woodlands and crofting settlements. The bleaker promontories of Rubha Mor and Rubha Reidh, though not of high intrinsic scenic merit in themselves, are visually inseparable from the mountain backdrop and only at Red Point does the rather plain local scene lose the advantage of this prospect.

OTHER NATIONAL INTERESTS

There are National Nature Reserves at Beinn Eighe and the Loch Maree Islands. Sites of Special Scientific Interest occur at An Teallach, Fionn Loch Islands, Letterewe Forest, Letterewe Oakwoods, Loch Shieldaig Woods, Liathach, Mheallaidh Wood, Coille-Creag-Loch, Beinn Bhan, Glas Cnoc. The Rassal Ashwood and Allt nan Carnan National Nature Reserves adjoin the southern limits of the area. The National Trust for Scotland has properties at Inverewe, Torridon and Shieldaig Island, and has entered into Conservation Agreements at Dundonnell Estate and Loch Shieldaig (Gairloch). The Forestry Commission owns land at Kinlochewe, Slattadale, Inverewe, Aultbea and Laide. The area also coincides partly with the existing National Park Direction Area.

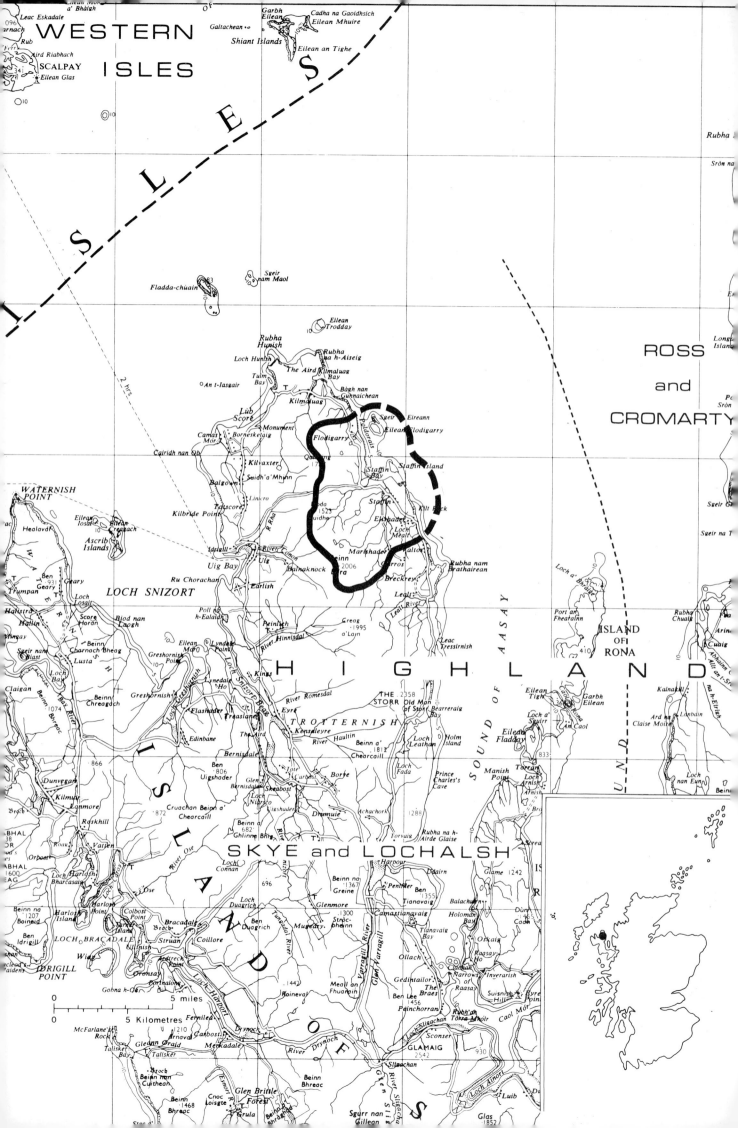

HIGHLAND REGION   TROTTERNISH

5,000 HECTARES

EXTENT OF AREA

This area extends from Flodigarry in the north to
Grealin in the south and includes the Quirang, Beinn
Edra and Staffin Island and Eilean Flodigarry. From
Drum nan Slochd in the north the landward margin
follows the scarp of Sgurr Mor south to Beinn Edra
and the Bealach Amadal. From there it swings due
east through Achnaguie, Grealin and Lonfearn to the
sea at Rubha nan Brathairean.

DESCRIPTION

The eastern aspect of the peninsula of Trotternish
affords an unusual landscape which combines the
spectacular scenery of landslip topography with the
fascination of columnar basaltic rock structures.
Huge masses of basalt have collapsed at the Quirang
to make a landscape of rock pinnacles interspersed
with moist green meadows and tiny lochans. Below
these strange formations lie peat moors and, on the
better land, crofting settlements with improved land
affording a green contrast to the brown moors. On
the seaward side the whole landscape drops
suddenly into the sea in cliffs of varying height, but
made up of more regular columnar formations of
basalt. These 'kilt rock' cliffs have occasional
waterfalls dropping sheer into the sea and afford
spectacular views over the Sound of Raasay to the
fjord coast of the mainland. The culmination of the
finest features of this north-eastern coast of Skye
centres on Staffin Bay, where the pattern of crofting
settlement is enclosed to the west by the spectacular
relief of the Quirang.

OTHER NATIONAL INTERESTS

The Quirang and Beinn Edra are two component
parts of the Trotternish Ridge Site of Special
Scientific Interest.

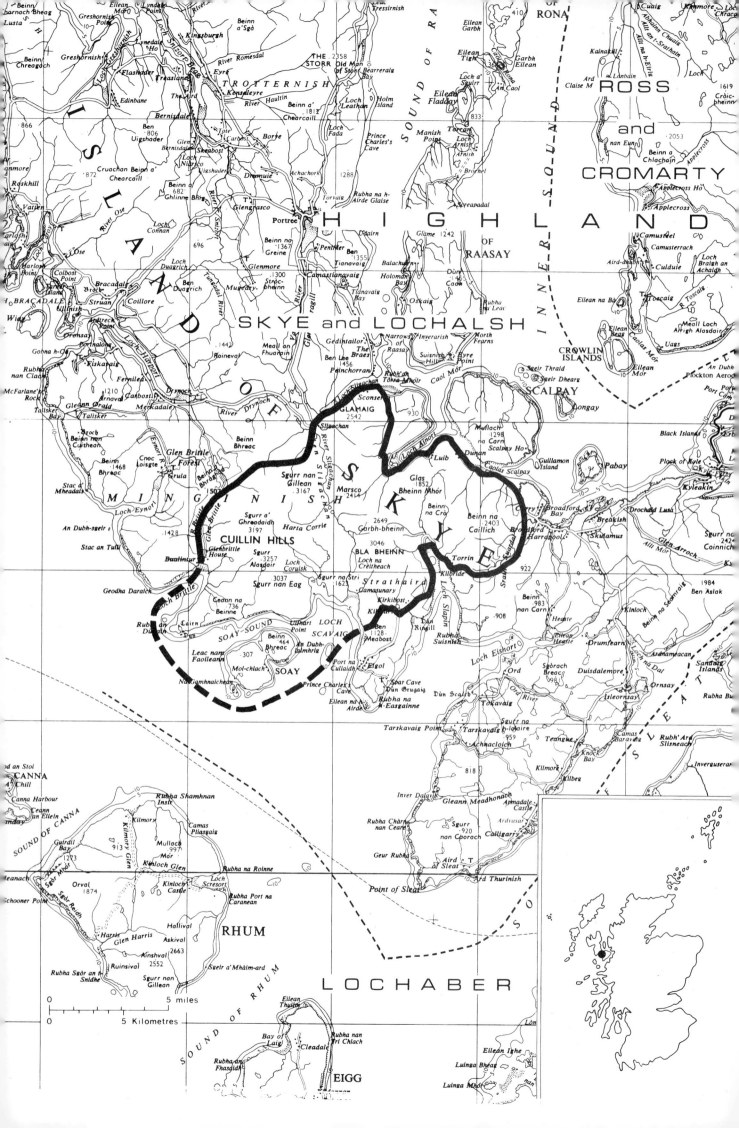

HIGHLAND REGION

THE CUILLIN HILLS

21,900 HECTARES

EXTENT OF AREA

The area includes the Black and Red Cuillin Hills,
Loch Scavaig and the Island of Soay. From
Sligachan the western limit of the area is identified by
the track through the Bealach a'Mhaim to Glen
Brittle, and in Glen Brittle by the lower eastern forest
edge. From Loch Brittle the seaward limits include
the Isle of Soay and much of Loch Scavaig where
Glen Scaladal has been identified as the southern
limit. From the head of that glen the Camusunary
tracks and the public road A861 to Suardal mark the
southern landward limits. From Suardal the track via
Coirechatachan to the public road A850 forms the
eastern limit, and the same public road continues to
Sligachan defining the remaining limits of the area.

DESCRIPTION

The jagged gabbro of the Black Cuillin, and smooth
pink granite of the Red Cuillin combine their
contrasting shapes to form a mountain area of
dramatic and distinctive outlines of great scenic
splendour. These remarkable hills contrive to
dominate much of the island seaboard of north-west
Scotland, making their presence felt in clear weather
from places as far apart as Ardnamurchan and Pairc
in Lewis. Closer at hand Sligachan is famous for its
view of the shapely and serrated Sgurr nan Gillean in
marked contrast to the pudding profiles of the Red
Cuillin to the east. Glen Brittle has magnificent
waterfalls, Torrin is dominated by the grey slabs of
Bla Bheinn, and Elgol provides the classic view of the
Black Cuillin in serried ranks about the concealed
amphitheatre of Loch Coruisk. The sharp-edged
ridges are scalloped by high corries in which lie small
lochans, but the lower slopes are also extremely
steep, bare and often scree-covered. The
surrounding U-shaped glaciated glens form a
contrast in their simplicity, and to seaward the Island
of Soay is a low, brown, heath-covered hump of
Torridonian sandstone, unspectacular, but providing
a further foil to the mountains in the wider setting of
Loch Scavaig.

OTHER NATIONAL INTERESTS

There are Sites of Special Scientific Interest at the
Cuillin Hills, Marsco, Sron a'Bhealain, Meall
a'Mhaoil, Strollamus, South West Strath and the
Elgol Coast. The Forestry Commission owns land at
Loch Slapin, Strath and Glen Brittle.

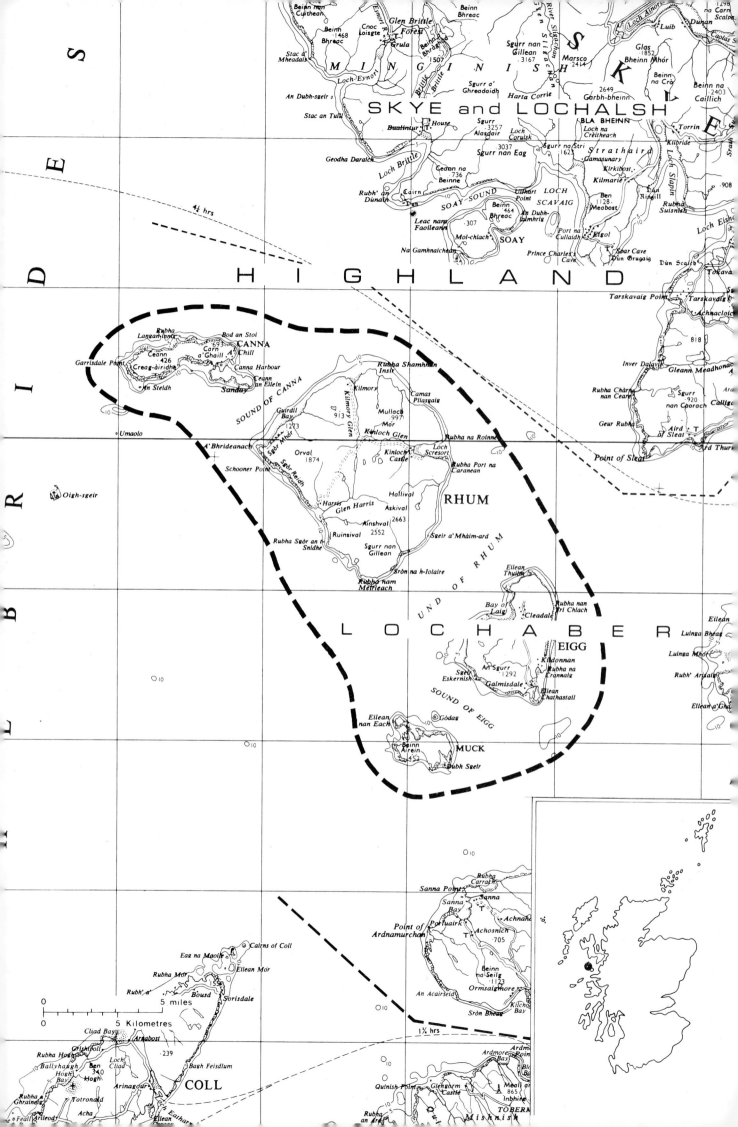

HIGHLAND REGION

THE SMALL ISLES

15,500 HECTARES

EXTENT OF AREA

The group of islands known as the Small Isles comprises Rhum, Eigg, Muck and Canna which form a compact group of contrasting islands within the wider coastal setting of the Cuillin of Skye, Morar, Moidart and Ardnamurchan.

DESCRIPTION

Each island has a different landscape character and outline that contrast one island with the next, and the sea inevitably plays an important role in setting off and linking the varying shapes of the islands, which make a major contribution to a seaboard of the highest scenic quality.

The scenery of Rhum contains within a small compass nearly all of the elements found in the other inner islands; brown, stepped country of Torridonian sandstone in the north, green grassy terraces separated by cliffs of basaltic lavas in the west, and steep slopes, sharp peaks, and knife-edged ridges in the south, where hard ultrabasic rocks have been carved like the Cuillin gabbro. Massive granite cliffs add yet another group of landforms around Bloodstone Hill, Glen Dibidil is a fine U-shaped valley, and at Kilmory is a stretch of machair and a small line of sand dunes. There is little cultivable land.

Basalt predominates on Eigg, giving good agricultural land, and a steep-sided ridge of Jurassic sandstone in the north forms impressive cliffs when viewed from the sea. At the southern end of the island the spectacular Sgurr of Eigg is a residual block of pitchstone lava which forms a long undulating ridge of bare grey rock and which, viewed on end, forms a flat-topped tower almost 400m above sea level. On the coast there is a series of large caves. There is a considerable amount of fertile ground, but natural woodland is confined to a few patches of hazel scrub, and mixed woodlands have been planted on the east side of the island.

Muck is a low island of Tertiary basalt giving a stepped profile, but having a rich soil and fine green pasture. The rock has been worn into cliffs and caves at sea level, more interesting than the low rocky headlands of the nearby mainland. Canna at the far end of the group is like Muck, but higher, with inland cliffs of reddish rock above grassy slopes, and a spectacular coastline of caves, arches and stacks carved from the basalt. The lower island of Sanday, linked by a bridge to Canna, contrasts with the higher ground, and has on it a church which forms a strong landscape feature on the seaward approach to Canna harbour.

OTHER NATIONAL INTERESTS

Rhum is a National Nature Reserve, and there are Sites of Special Scientific Interest on Muck, Canna and Eigg, where there is also an extensive Scottish Wildlife Trust Reserve.

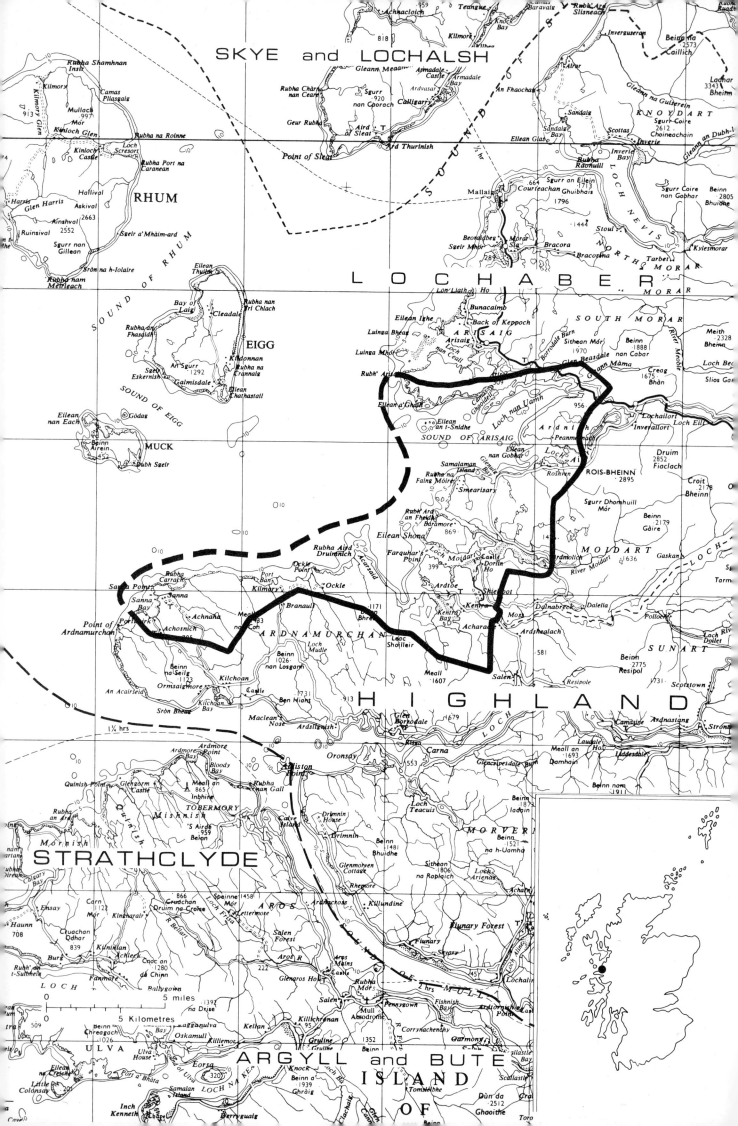

HIGHLAND REGION

13,500 HECTARES

EXTENT OF AREA

This essentially coastal area extends from the south shore of the Morar Peninsula to include the Sound of Arisaig, Loch Moidart, Kentra Bay and the northern shore of Ardnamurchan. There is a strong visual inter-relationship with the Small Isles. The seaward margin approximates to a line drawn from Rubha Arisaig south-westwards to Sgurr na Meann on the south shore of Sanna Bay in Ardnamurchan. From there the watershed between the north and south slopes of the peninsula serves to define the southern landward margin of the area as far as Beinn nan Leathaid above Achateny. Due east across the Achateny glen the watershed is resumed from the summit of Tom na Gainmheich as far east as the summit of Conach Bhreac above Acharacle. From there the eastern limit of the area runs due north to the public roads B8044 and B850 as far as Blain, then northwards to Beinn Bhreac and eastwards to Ard Molach. From Ard Molach the eastward margin is defined by an arbitrary line running east of due north to Eilean Buidhe in Loch Ailort and then along the summit of the ridge An-t-aonach on the west side of the inner reach of Loch Ailort, meeting the railway at Loch Dubh. The railway defines the northern limits of the area as far west as Torr-an-t-Sagairt, whence the ridge line via Doire Fhada is followed to Rubha Arisaig.

DESCRIPTION

The area exhibits a coastal landscape of great diversity and interest, in places enhanced by the mountain background, although it is the coastal fringe that is considered to be outstanding. This coastal fringe is made up of four main subsidiary areas each with a character of its own, but complementing the others and all linked together by views of the enhancing offshore islands of the Small Isles. The indented rocky coastline of northern Ardnamurchan with its succeeding bays and headlands affords fine views from each successive glen, aligned as they are in the direction of the Small Isles, with oblique views across to the sands and hills of Morar. The volcanic landforms contribute greatly to the character of this shore. Across the flat sandy bay and moss of Kentra, the steep wooded enclosing slopes of Loch Moidart offer a contrast. This is a sheltered, introverted landscape of intimate seclusion and charm, so closed in upon itself that the rounded forms of the wooded islands amongst the braided channels of the loch reveal vista after vista of water, sand, rock, woodland and grassland in ever-changing western light.

Loch Ailort and Loch nan Uamh are more open in aspect, again with fine views to the Small Isles, but in the foreground is a richly wooded shore of rocky promontories, while the waters of the lochs are studded with heather and scrub-covered islets which do not frame the view as in Loch Moidart, but are an

MORAR, MOIDART AND ARDNAMURCHAN

enhancing element in the wider prospect. This richly patterned western prospect typifies for many people the scenery they associate with the romance of 'the Road to the Isles.'

OTHER NATIONAL INTERESTS

The Forestry Commission owns land at Roshven, Ardmolach, and Arivegaig. There are Sites of Special Scientific Interest at Ardnamurchan, Kentra Bay and Moss, Loch Moidart, and Glen Beasdale.

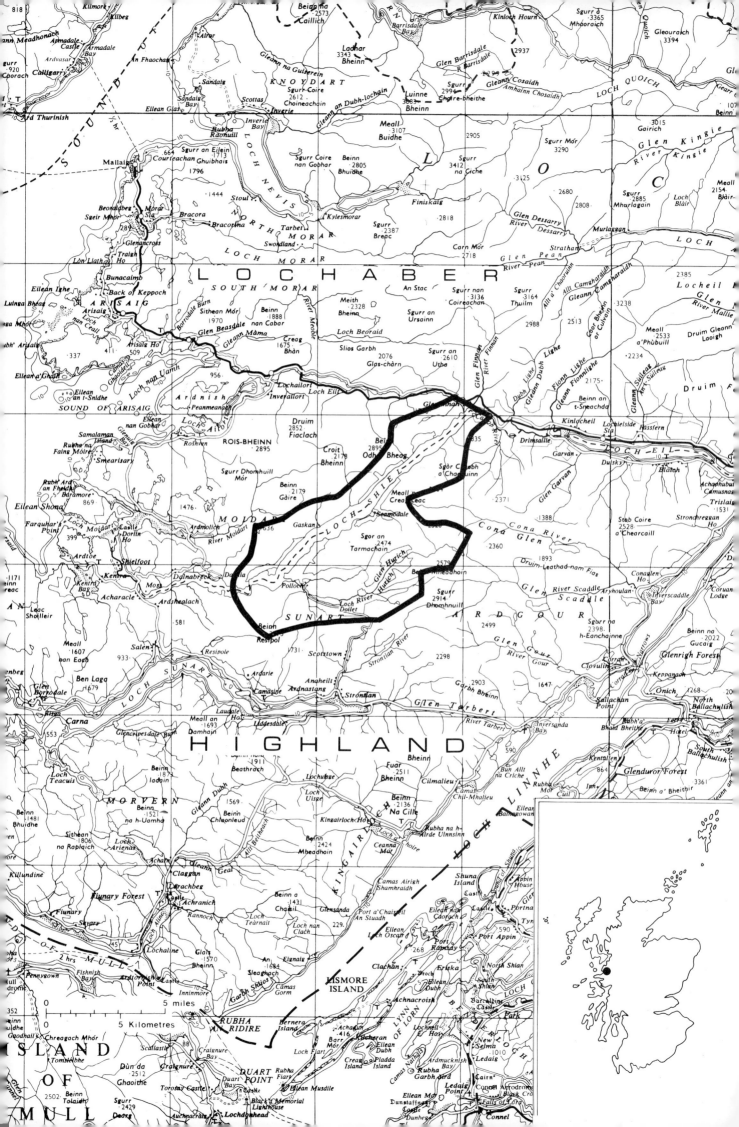

HIGHLAND REGION   LOCH SHIEL

13,400 HECTARES

EXTENT OF AREA

This area includes the entrenched fjord-like part of
Loch Shiel and the side glen of Glenhurich in
Ardgour. Its western limit is defined by the Creagan
an Fhithich ridge rising above Eilean Fhionain at the
point where the loch swings westwards towards
Acharacle, following the summits of the hills on the
western flank of the loch. Creag nan Lochan (498m),
Beinn an t-Samhainn (525m), Beinn Odhar Beag,
Beinn Odhar Mhor (870m), An-t-Sleubhaich, an
outlier of the last, to the public road A803(T) where it
bridges the railway west of Glenfinnan. The road
defines the northern boundary as far east as the
north shoulder of Meall na-h-Airigh (480m), where
the summits extending in a southerly direction of
Sgurr Caobh a'Chaoruinn, Meall nan Creag Leac,
Stob a Chuir and Carn na Nathrach to Druim Garbh,
identify the eastern margin. The ridge west from
Druim Glas to Beinn Resipol (845m) forms the
southern limits, regaining the loch at Crudh' an Eich
near Achanellan.

DESCRIPTION

Loch Shiel separates Moidart from Ardgour. Seen
from Glenfinnan it presents the unity of appearance
of a deep fjord winding its way between the
interlocking spurs of precipitous mountains. The
lowest slopes of these interlocking ridges are
sometimes bare grass and rock, sometimes mantled
in woodland, some of it planted conifers, some of it
native oak. Beneath the high peak of Ben Resipol the
loch twists out of its highland grandeur into a gentler
lowland moss landscape, but before it does so its
character is enriched by Eilean Fhianain, the
narrows of the Linne Gorm, and the wooded bay at
the foot of Glenhurich, a deep, remote, now heavily
afforested glen, with a fine river and loch, Loch
Doilet, enclosed by the rugged Ardgour Hills. The
fine receding views along the sinuous trench of the
loch are perhaps further enhanced for many people
by the strong historical associations with the
Macdonalds, and their role in the Jacobite uprising.

OTHER NATIONAL INTERESTS

The Forestry Commission owns land at Glenhurich
and Glenfinnan, and Loch Shiel is a Site of Special
Scientific Interest.

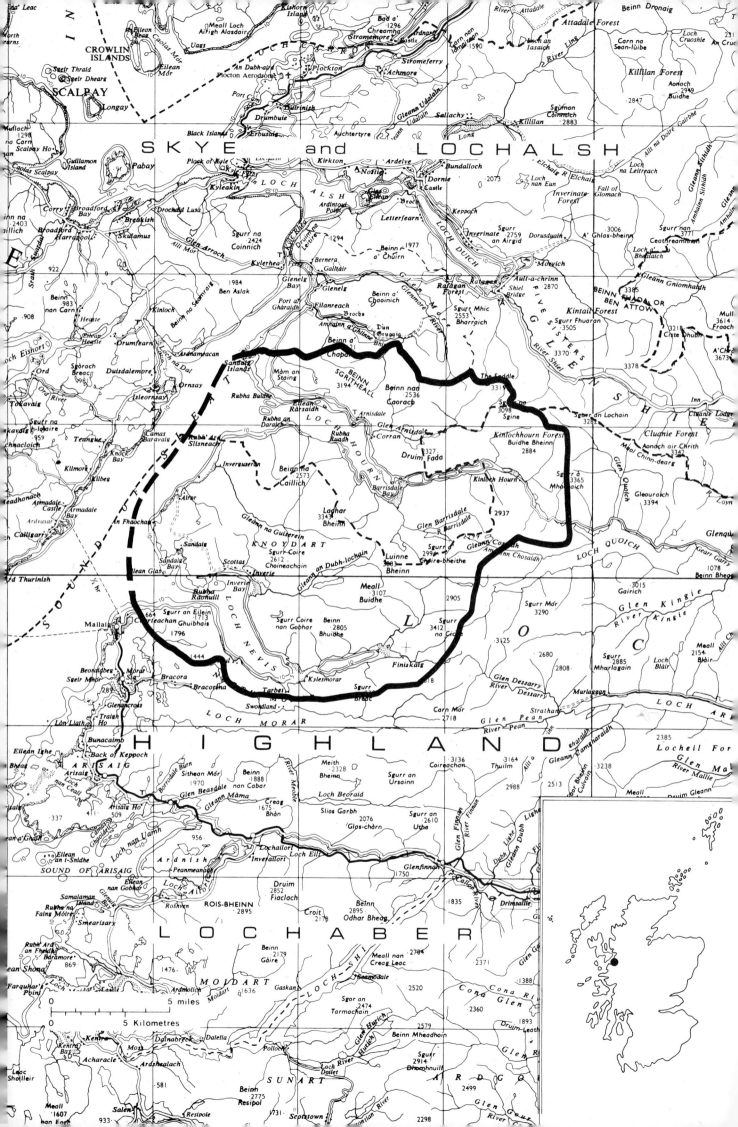

HIGHLAND REGION   KNOYDART

39,500 HECTARES

EXTENT OF AREA

The area includes Loch Nevis, Knoydart, Loch
Hourn, Beinn Sgritheall (974m) and Glen Arnisdale.
Seaward the margin runs from Sandaig to
Mallaigvaig. From Mallaigvaig the southern margin
turns east via the ridge of Carn Mhic Ghille-chaim to
the summit ridge south of Stoul where it follows the
watershed between Loch Nevis and Loch Morar
eastwards to Sgurr na h-Aide (859m). From there the
eastern margin strikes north eastward past Sgurr na
Ciche (1040m) to Sgurr a'Chlaidheimh and Sron Lice
na Fearna above Loch Quoich and the pass to
Kinlochhourn. From here the northern limit is
identified by a line of peaks separating the glens of
the Loch Hourn basin from Glen Shiel and
culminating in the Saddle (1010m). West of the
Saddle Gleann Aoidhdailean and Beinn a'Chaipuil
and the Sandaig River define the northern limits of
the area.

DESCRIPTION

 The outstanding scenic value of this area derives
from the penetration by sea lochs deep into remote
and rugged mountain country that has experienced
intense glaciation. The extensive coastline
contributes significantly to the character of the area,
as do the deep glens carved between high graceful
peaks, with the intervening ground broken by rocky
crags.
   Loch Nevis and Loch Hourn are archetypal
western sea lochs, wide outer lochs separated by
narrows from narrow inner lochs. Both penetrate the
mountain mass but they differ in character. Loch
Hourn is reminiscent of a Norwegian fjord, especially
in its sombre inner reach, while Loch Nevis is lighter
and more open, thanks to the lower hills on its
southern flank. The bays of Loch Nevis add interest
to the southern shore of Knoydart, but equally
important are the soaring peaks like Sgurr na Ciche
which ring the head of the loch. Loch Hourn is
entrenched between steeper and more massive
mountains, Beinn Sgritheall to the north, and Ladhar
Bheinn with its corries to the south. Looking west
from both lochs, and from the intervening coast of
Knoydart, there are magnificent views of Skye and
the Small Isles.
   From coastal features of elevated cliff lines and
terraces, the deep glens of Knoydart run inland,
often with stepped long profiles, so that broad
marshy flats or lochans alternate with steep wooded
gorges. Despite the roughness of the ground, the
hills are shapely and well defined, the peaks almost
bare of vegetation, while the slopes carry bracken,
grass and sedge, the more precipitous parts often
wooded with birch, ash and oak. It is one of the most
remote inhabited parts of Scotland. This remoteness,
together with its extreme ruggedness and fine
coastline and sea-lochs, make the Rough Bounds of
Knoydart one of the wildest and most beautiful parts
of mainland Scotland.

OTHER NATIONAL INTERESTS

The Forestry Commission owns land at Eileanreach
Forest, and there are Sites of Special Scientific
Interest at Coille Mhialairigh (Loch Hourn), Loch
Nevis and the Mallaig Coast.

41

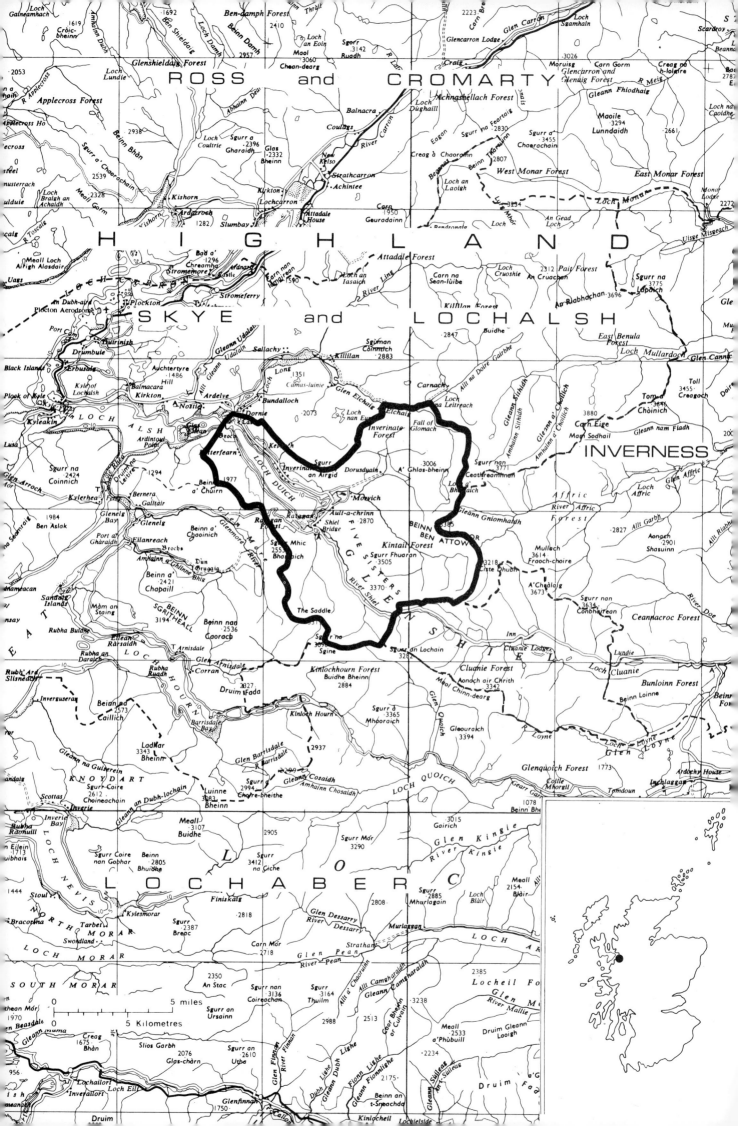

HIGHLAND REGION   KINTAIL

15,500 HECTARES

EXTENT OF AREA

This area includes lower Glen Shiel, the Kintail
Forest, Beinn Fhada, the Falls of Glomach, Glen
Lichd and Loch Duich. From Totaig at the mouth of
Loch Duich the western limit is defined by the ridge
of Faire Donn and the watershed of Ratagan, as far
south as the Saddle. In the vicinity of the Saddle
between Spidean Dhomnuill Bhric (940m) and Sgurr
a'Bhac Chaolais (885m) the margin runs with that of
the proposed national scenic area of Knoydart. From
there it runs via the summit of Creag nan Damh to the
east boundary of the National Trust for Scotland
property of Kintail. This property boundary is
followed north to Glen Elchaig, along the River
Elchaig and its tributary, the Eas Ban in Coire nan
Gall, to regain the summit ridge on the north flank of
Loch Duich which is followed to Eilean Donan and
Totaig.

DESCRIPTION

Three long mountain ranges terminate around the
head of Loch Duich: Beinn Fhada, the Five Sisters of
Kintail, and the Cluanie Forest which culminates in
the Saddle. The glens which radiate from Loch Duich
between these mountains, which form the watershed
of mainland Scotland within a few miles of the
western sea, are short, steepsided and deep. They
contain burns or rivers which rush and tumble
through waterfalls and pools girt with alder to flow
through pastures in the lower glens, while high
corries and ridges contain their upper reaches. It is
the grandeur of the mountains that makes the
scenery here so magnificent. Glen Shiel is dominated
by the pinnacles of the Saddle and the spearlike
cone of Faochag. The Five Sisters of Kintail, when
viewed from Mam Ratagan, Letterfearn or Carr Brae,
are supremely elegant peaks, forming a graceful and
imposing background at the head of Loch Duich.
The serrated ridge of massive Beinn Fhada towers
over Glen Lichd and Glen Choinneachan. W. H.
Murray (1963) has written: 'In Kintail nothing lacks;
all things culminate. It is the epitome of the West
Highland scene.'

OTHER NATIONAL INTERESTS

The National Trust for Scotland has properties at
Kintail, Morvich and Falls of Glomach, and the
Forestry Commission owns land at Ratagan, Glen
Lichd and Inverinate. There is a Site of Special
Scientific Interest at the Falls of Glomach.

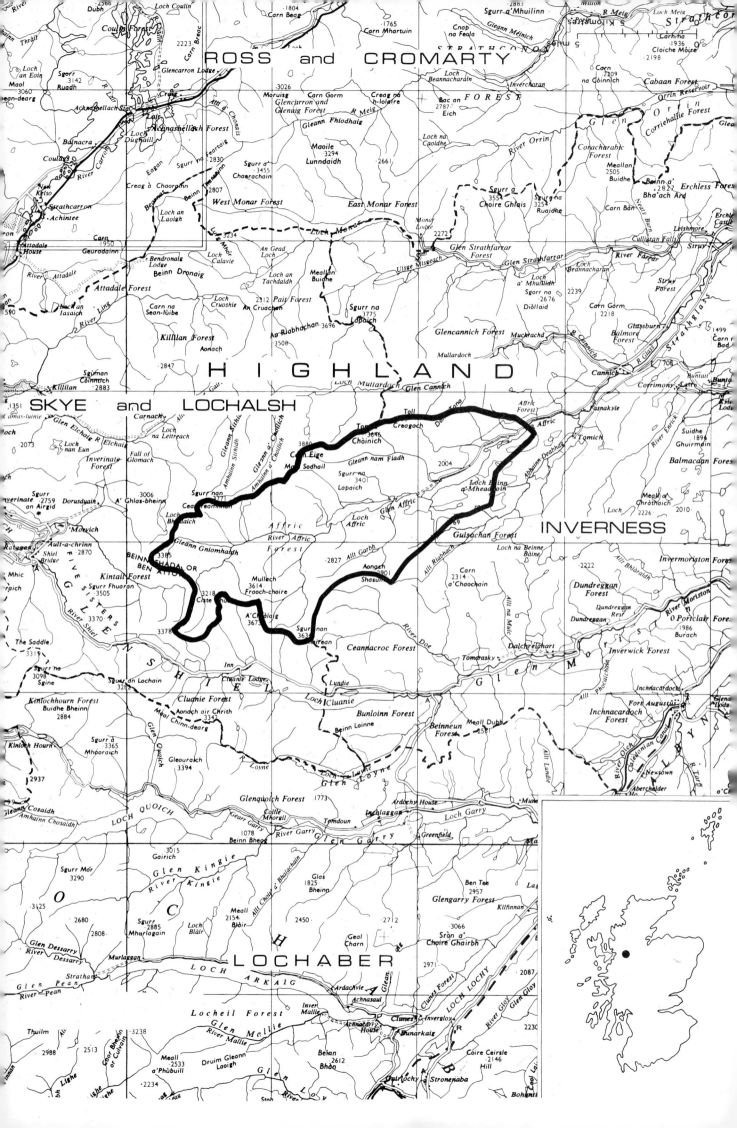

HIGHLAND REGION　　GLEN AFFRIC

19,300 HECTARES

EXTENT OF AREA

The area covers all of Glen Affric west of the dam impounding Loch Beinn a'Mheadhoin. From Sgurr Gaorsaic at the western extremity of the glen the limits of the area coincide with those of the proposed national scenic area of Kintail, here formed by the National Trust for Scotland property boundary. From Sgurr a'Bhealaich Dheirg, on the watershed between Glen Affric (Fionngleann) and Glen Shiel, the southern limit follows the watershed eastwards via Ciste Dubh, an outlier of Mullach Fraoch Choire and Sgurr nan Conbhairean (1109m) to the watershed between Glen Affric and Glen Guisachan, which is not included, as far as the dam. From the dam the principal watershed between Glen Affric and Glen Cannich forms the northern boundary, and traverses the summits of Toll Creagach, Tom a'Choinnich, Carn Eige (1183m), Mam Sodhail (1181m) and Sgurr nan Ceathreamhnan (1151m), back to Sgurr Gaorsaic and Beinn Fhada.

DESCRIPTION

Glen Affric is flanked on the north by the highest mountains of the North West Highlands, shapely conical peaks ranged above a long glaciated valley, with steep sides and a broad floor in which are set two great lochs and a river. The lower slopes of the hills are clothed in forest, one of the most beautiful remnants of native Caledonian Pine forest, with a leavening of birches and a sufficiently open canopy to permit the growth of heather and blaeberry. Glen Affric is often cited as Scotland's loveliest glen. From the rich woodland at the dam to the stark mountains of the upper glen, where all is moor and heather, it displays a fine variety of glen scenery. Fiona Leney, writing of the area in 1974, caught the essence of the place: '. . . . the area maintains a sense of wilderness, less rugged than the remote area of North West Scotland and has a grandeur and classic beauty that is not found in the bleaker lands to the north.'

OTHER NATIONAL INTERESTS

Much of the area lies within the Forestry Commission's Glen Affric Forest, and all of it within the existing National Park Direction Area. There are Sites of Special Scientific Interest in the Affric-Cannich Hills and in Glen Affric.

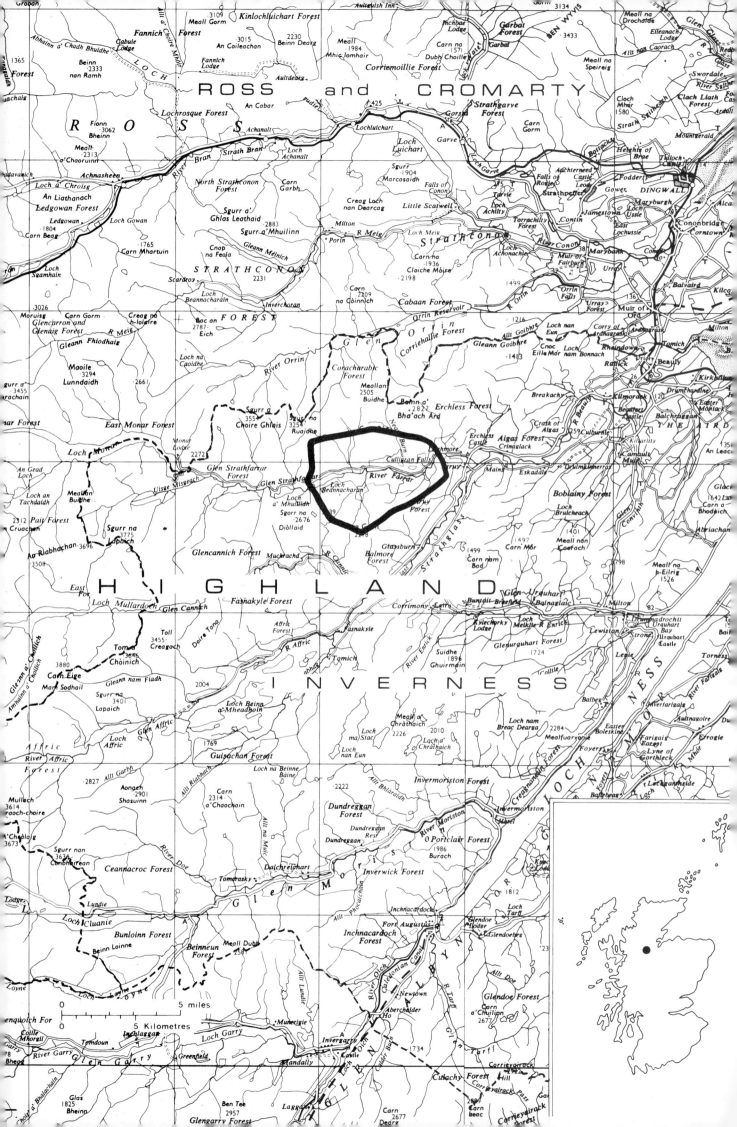

HIGHLAND REGION

GLEN STRATHFARRAR

3,800 HECTARES

EXTENT OF AREA

The area covers only the middle section of Glen
Strathfarrar from Culligran Falls in the east to the
head of Loch Beannacharan in the west. The
summits of Garbh-charn (854m) and Carn Ban define
the northern margin, while those of Meall
a'Mhadaidh (682m), Carn Gorm and Carn Moraig
identify the southern limit.

DESCRIPTION

Three great glens feed into Strathglass and the
Beauly River: Glen Strathfarrar, Glen Cannich and
Glen Affric. Of these the last has already been
described. All three are in the form of long deep
troughs, studded with lochs, declining eastwards
from high mountains and becoming avenues of
wooded verdure while still flanked by lofty skylines.
In scenic terms, all three have been adversely
affected by hydro-electric schemes, Glen Cannich
and Glen Strathfarrar more so than Glen Affric.
Neither of these two northern glens attains the
excellence of Glen Affric, with the exception of the
lower middle portion of Strathfarrar. Here the
sinuous steepsided glen is enhanced by its shining
river and extensive natural pine woodland. Loch
Beannacharan offers a calm contrast to the river, the
rushing waters of which finally plunge over the
Culligran Falls into the lower strath.

OTHER NATIONAL INTERESTS

The area lies within the existing National Park
Direction Area. Part of the Glen Strathfarrar National
Nature Reserve lies within the area, as does part of
the Glenstrathfarrar Site of Special Scientific
Interest.

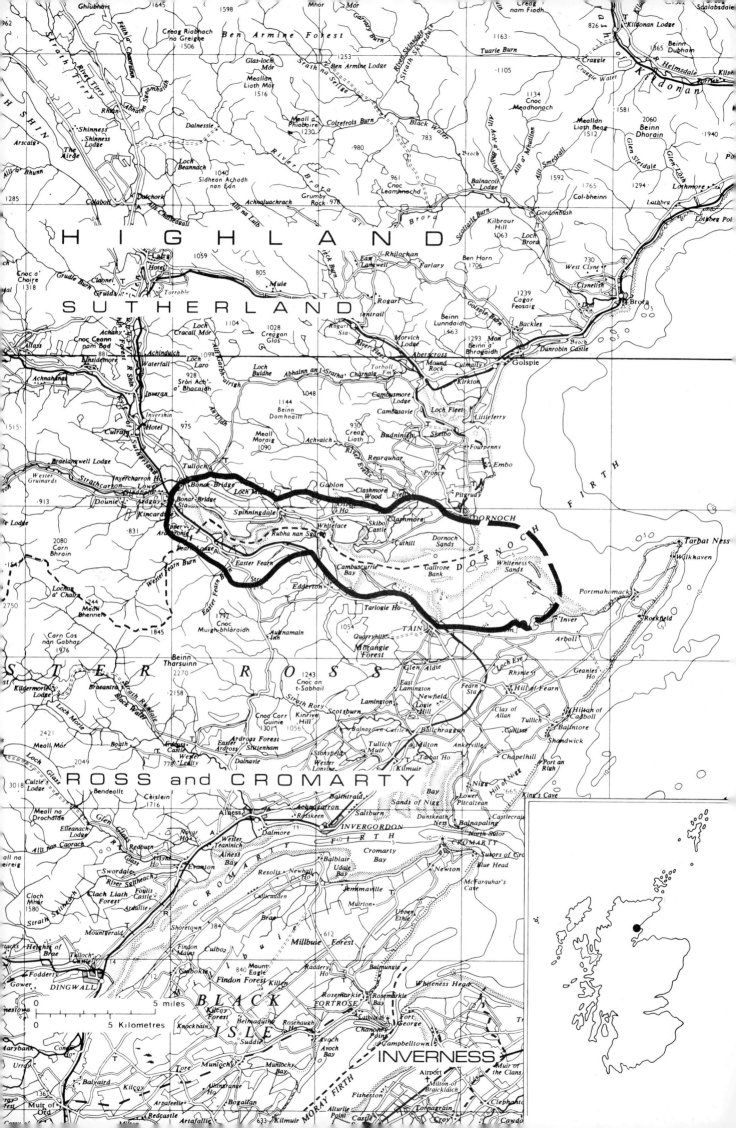

HIGHLAND REGION   DORNOCH FIRTH

7,500 HECTARES

EXTENT OF AREA

The area includes the whole of the Firth below Bonar
Bridge, Migdale and the Morrich More. From Bonar
Bridge the western extent of the area is defined by
the public road A9(T) south to Ardgay. From Ardgay
the western margin ascends Church Hill via Oldtown
to run eastwards from Cnoc Bad-a-bhacaidh, Cnoc
a'Chlaiginn, Cnoc an Liath-bhaid to Struie Hill. From
the foot of Struie Hill (330m) the limit is defined by
the railway along the south shore of the Firth to the
mouth of the River Tain. Between the River Tain and
Inver Bay, the southern boundary of the Morrich
More SSSI is adopted. The seaward limits include
Innis Mhor and strike ashore to skirt the southern
fringes of Dornoch taking up the line of the public
road A9(T) at Drumdivan. The trunk road is followed
westwards to the unclassified road to Acharry Moor,
Claiseanglas and Migdale, and on to Bonar Bridge.

DESCRIPTION

By comparison with other east coast firths the
Dornoch Firth is narrow and sinuous, yet it exhibits
within its compass a surprising variety of landscapes.
It is enclosed by abrupt rounded granitic hills clad in
heather moor and scree, their Gaelic names of *cnoc,
meall* and *creag* giving the clue to their character.
Their lower slopes are frequently wooded, oakwoods
being a noticeable feature of the area, but with other
deciduous and coniferous species represented in
plantations which vary from the policy plantings of
Skibo Castle to the pines of the Struie Forest.
Interspersed among these hills and plantations are
areas of pasture and arable on the lower alluvial
lands, with whin and broom a common feature in the
hedgerows and on the sandy links of the outer firth.
But above all it is the firth itself, with its innumerable
bays, sands, flats, shallows and promontories which
presents a constantly changing scene as much with
the coming and going of the tide as with the
changing scene afforded by passage round its
shores. Migdale with its loch expresses an inland
variation of the same theme and has been included
for the complement it makes to the firth, the last
undeveloped estuary of its kind on the east coast.

OTHER NATIONAL INTERESTS

The Forestry Commission owns land at Struie,
Davochfin and Morrich More and there are Sites of
Special Scientific Interest at Morrich More, Easter
Fearn, Migdale Rock, Ledmore Wood and in the
Lower Dornoch Firth.

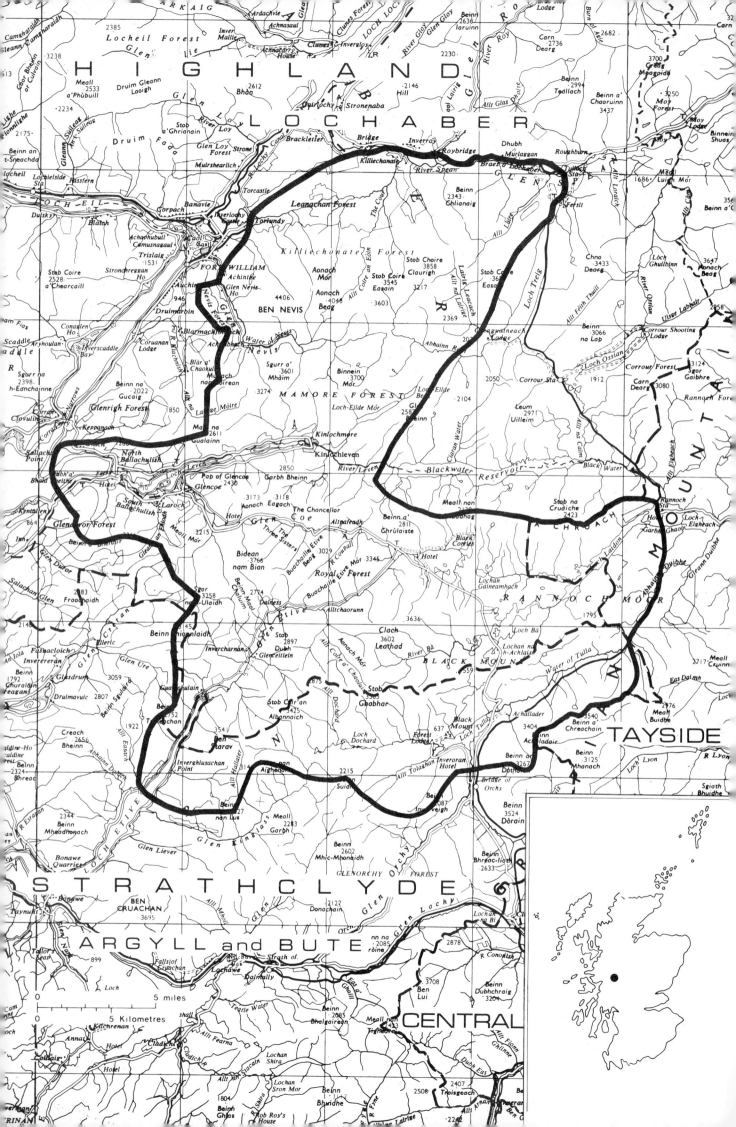

HIGHLAND REGION

BEN NEVIS AND GLEN COE

79,600 HECTARES — HIGHLAND REGION
17,500 HECTARES — STRATHCLYDE REGION
4,500 HECTARES — TAYSIDE REGION

EXTENT OF AREA

This western Grampian Mountains area extends from Glen Spean in the north to Glen Kinglass in the south, and from Rannoch Station in the east to the mouth of Loch Leven in the west. It straddles three regions, Highland, Strathclyde and Tayside, the largest portion being in Highland, and is therefore described here.

From Fort William, which is not included in the area, the western limit follows the ridge of the Nevis Forest on the west flank of Glen Nevis to the summit of Mullach nan Coirean. From there it follows the ridge of Mam na Gualainn, Tom Meadhoin and Beinn an Aonaich Mhoir to Rubha Cuil-cheanna on Loch Linnhe. Across the mouth of Loch Leven it follows the west slope of Beinn a'Bheithir (1001m) and on to Sgorr a'Choise, Corr na Beinne, Beinn Fhionnlaidh and Beinn Trilleachan above Loch Etive. At Rubha Bharr on Loch Etive the southern margin crosses to Ardmaddy Bay, and follows the northern flank of Glen Kinglass through the summits of Beinn nan Lus, Beinn nan Aighenan, Beinn Suidhe, Beinn Inverveigh, Beinn an Dothaidh to Beinn Achaladair (1038m). At this point the existing National Park Direction Area boundary is resumed as far as Rannoch Station. From Rannoch Station the ridge A'Chruach is followed westwards as far as Beinn a'Chrulaiste where the limits are defined in a northerly direction through Glas Bheinn, and the eastern Stob Coire Easain to Beinn Chlianaig. From this hill the southern boundary of the Leanachan Forest and the electricity pylon line from Torlundy to Claggan are used to identify the limits of the area.

DESCRIPTION

There is a great variety of landform and scenery within this area, attributable in the main to the intricacy of its geological structure. Granite outcrops form the dominant features around Ben Nevis, Glen Etive and Rannoch Moor, while Glencoe is of volcanic origin. The variety of scenery throughout the area is witnessed in hills that may be smooth or jagged, rounded or precipitous, grass or heather covered. The glens may contain moorland, meadow, arable or forest, and swift streams or calm lochs. The sea shore may be wooded and bayed as in outer Loch Leven, or fjord-like as in the inner loch and Loch Etive.

Many people would consider that Glen Nevis ranks with Glen Affric and Glen Lyon as one of the most beautiful glens in Scotland. No other part of the country has greater relative relief. But it is not scale alone which makes Glen Nevis memorable. The lower reaches are pastoral, with an alder threaded river and woodlands clothing the glen sides. The middle section exhibits a 'Himalayan' character, while the upper glen is a place of peaceful meadows, Alpine in feeling, enhanced by the presence of the graceful Steall waterfall. On the north side of Ben Nevis is Coire Leis, '. . . . the most splendid of all Scottish corries' (Murray).

South of the Mamore Forest lies the fjord-like trench of Loch Leven. The soaring mountain walls rising from the deciduous wooded shores of the deep and narrow waters of the inner loch give it a character not replicated elsewhere in Scotland. Its beauty is further enhanced by the islands at the mouth of Glen Coe, and by the swift tidal race which flows through the narrows at Ballachulish below the sharp cones of Beinn a'Bheithir.

Glen Coe itself '. . . . must rank high among the most spectacular scenic experiences in Scotland' (Whittow). Lying between the 6 mile-long notched ridge of Aonach Eagach and the truncated spurs of Bidean nam Bian, the highest mountain in Argyll (1141m), the glen is an ice worn valley mantled with screes and debris from the mountains. The place called The Study offers impressive vistas of the Three Sisters. Here the River Coe flows westwards over foaming cascades and through clear pools to the calm waters of Loch Achtriochtan. The peaty flats of the lower glen are in sharp contrast to the towering precipices and waterfalls around them.

Glen Etive is not of the same awe-inspiring grandeur, but nevertheless it is a deep cleft through towering peaks, notably the portal peaks of the Buachailles and the great slabs of Ben Starav. The River Etive with its numerous waterfalls is an important feature of the glen. To the east lies Rannoch Moor, probably the best known moor in Scotland. Its sometimes endless-seeming wastes have a beauty derived from the inter-relationship of water and islands with the moor, and the relationship of the moor to its surrounding mountains.

OTHER NATIONAL INTERESTS

There is a National Nature Reserve at Rannoch Moor and Sites of Special Scientific Interest at Rannoch Moor, Crannach Wood, Doire Darach, Ard Trilleachan, Bidean nam Bian, Carnach Wood, Camas Calltuinn, St. Johns Church, Callert, Ben Nevis and Lon Lianachain. Part of the Glen Roy SSSI extends into Glen Spean in the north eastern extremity of the area. The Forestry Commission owns land in Glen Spean, at Leanachan, in Glen Nevis, at Ballachulish and Glen Coe, in Glen Etive and on Rannoch Moor. The National Trust for Scotland has property in Glen Coe. The area is less extensive than and is contained within the existing National Park Direction Area.

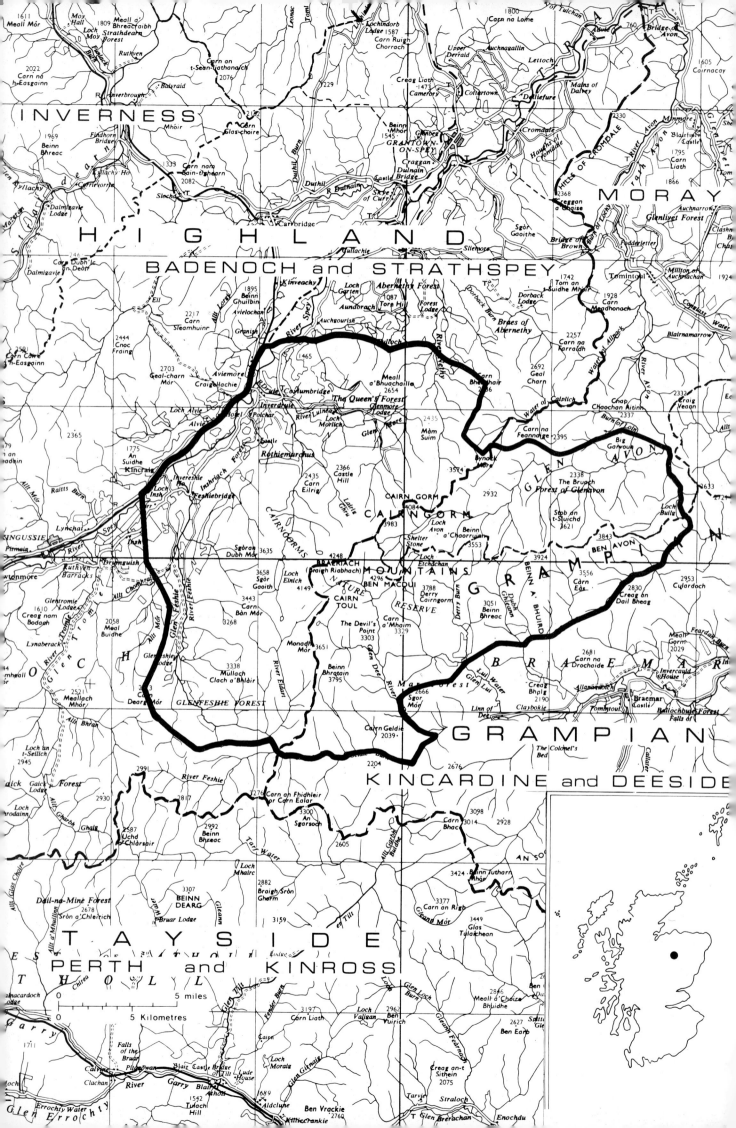

HIGHLAND REGION

37,400 HECTARES — HIGHLAND REGION
29,800 HECTARES — GRAMPIAN REGION

EXTENT OF AREA

This area lies partly in Highland Region and partly in Grampian Region, but as the greater part of it falls within the former it is dealt with here. It extends from Glen Feshie in the west to Glen Builg in the east and from Pityoulish and Ryvoan in the north to the Geldie Burn in the south, and covers the principal summits of the Cairngorm Plateau. From the River Spey at Dalfaber the western margin is defined by the railway as far south as Dunachton, whence a line drawn through the summits of Creag Dubh, Creag na Sroine, Carn Dearg Beag, Carn Dearg Mor (857m), and Carn an Fhidhleir Lorgaidh on the west flank of Glen Feshie, identifies the western extent of the area. From Carn an Fhidhleir Lorgaidh and Sron na Ban-righ the southern limit is along the course of the Geldie Burn to Chest of Dee and up the course of the Dee to strike east over Sgor Mor and Sgor Dubh and across Glen Lui to Meall an Lundain. From this summit the series of lateral meltwater channels defining the edge of the high plateau, and in which the headwaters of the Quoich and Gairn rise, is followed as far as Loch Builg. Glen Builg forms the eastern margin as far as the confluence of the Builg with the Avon, whence the ridge along the north flank of Glen Avon forms the northern limit of the area as far west as Coire Odhar of Bynack More (1090m). From here the existing National Park Direction Area boundary west to Pityoulish defines the remainder of the northern limit.

DESCRIPTION

The granite plateau of the Cairngorm Mountains forms the most extensive area of land above 1,000 metres anywhere in Britain. Its height is less immediately apparent than its bulk, but there are four summits over 1,200 metres (Cairngorm, Ben Macdhui, Cairn Toul and Braeriach) while three others, Cairn Lochan, Beinn a'Bhuird and Ben Avon are nearly so. The high plateau is bleak and bare and it is the immensity of scale, once realised, which impresses. Its edges are glacially sculptured into huge corries which excel in grandeur anything to be found elsewhere in Scotland, with the exception of Coire Leis of Ben Nevis. This scale '. . . . with the vast corries, the massive slopes, the long passes, the wide skies, and the very bareness of the ground, where the elements work with a power not known at lower altitudes, gives to these plateaux their distinctive quality.' (Murray, 1962).

The edge of the plateau, where not etched by corries, is well defined by long smooth steep slopes which, seen from Speyside or Deeside, rise in tiers. Snow lies for a long time at the top of these slopes. Lower down, deer forest, sheep grazing and forestry assume a greater importance in the appearance of the landscape. It is the forests around the plateau foot which for many people characterise the Cairngorm Mountains; three extensive and differing

THE CAIRNGORM MOUNTAINS

remnants of the native Caledonian Pine Forest occur at Rothiemurchus and Abernethy, Glen Feshie, and Mar.

In Rothiemurchus the pines on the upper forest slopes give way to a mixture of pine and birch, and then to the rich policy woodlands of Strathspey. The forests are deeply carpeted with heather, blaeberry and other flora, and the woods are interspersed with lochans of varying character, and views culminating in the peaty waters of the Spey itself.

Glen Feshie is wilder and sterner, the pines mature and solitary, interspersed with juniper. The river dominates in this forest, a great, braided, mountain stream with shingle beds cast over an uneven flood plain, almost continental in scale.

Mar Forest is different yet again. Higher, and therefore less rich than Rothiemurchus in its flora, it graduates from birch, pine, and fir to massive pines alone, again with a ground cover of heather and blaeberry. Like Glen Feshie the rivers are important here but not for their scale and grandeur. They are noisy burns dashing over granite boulders washed brightly pink by their clear waters, a lively element in the landscape. These wooded flanks of the Cairngorm plateau form a setting of rare beauty for the mountain massif, and are in turn enhanced by the mountain backdrop.

OTHER NATIONAL INTERESTS

The area contains the Cairngorm National Nature Reserve, and Sites of Special Scientific Interest in the Eastern Cairngorms, and at Inchrory, Abernethy Forest, Alvie, and at the River Spey-Insh Marshes where there is an R.S.P.B. reserve. The Glen More Forest Park as well as parts of the Queens Forest and Inshriach Forest lie within the area. The existing National Park Direction Area is also contained within the proposed area. There is a Scottish Wildlife Trust Reserve at Pass of Ryvoan.

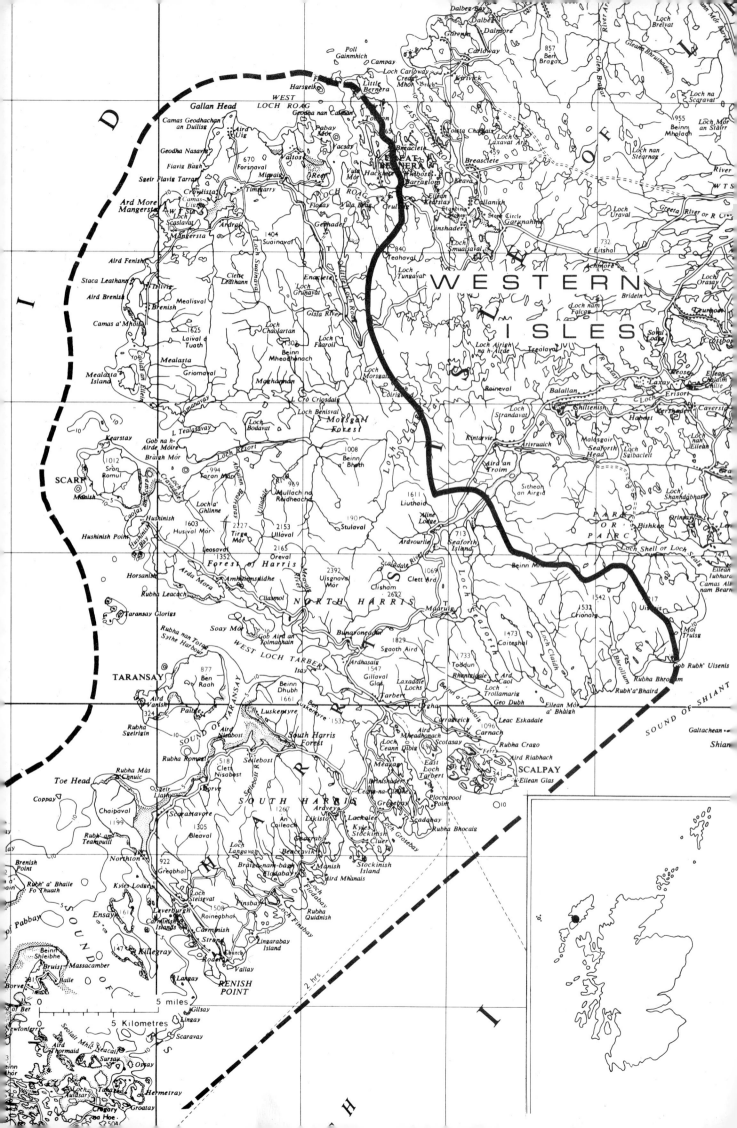

WESTERN ISLES ISLANDS AREA

109,600 HECTARES

SOUTH LEWIS, HARRIS AND NORTH UIST

EXTENT OF AREA

This extensive area stretches from Valtos in the north to Loch Eport in the south, and covers the mountainous parts of south west Lewis, all of Harris, the Sound of Harris and the northern part of North Uist which forms a backdrop to the sound and its islands. The eastern and western limits are across open sea, but the northern margin is defined by a line enclosing the western flank of Great Bernera, the eastern flank of Little Loch Roag and running south through the summits of the Caultrashals, Ascleit, Kearnaval, Beinn a'Mhuil, Beinn Mhor (572m), Gormol, and Uisenis and on to the headland of Gob Rubh'Uisenis on the Sound of Shiant. The southern limit is defined by Loch Eport as far west as Bay Sonish and then north westwards by Loch Scadavay and the summits of Marrogh, Marrival (230m) and Clettraval to Griminish Point.

DESCRIPTION

There is a striking contrast between the subdued topography of most of Lewis and the bold rugged hills of South Lewis and Harris which, viewed from the north, rise abruptly out of an expanse of blanket bog. Around the rugged hills, there are a number of different contrasting lowland and coastal landscapes. These have been identified as knock-and-lochan, rocky indented coast, and wide sandy machair beaches contained between rocky headlands. Each type has elements of its own which combine to produce landscapes with a variety of form, colour and grain, which are further diversified by changes of scale and aspect.

North Harris has the highest peaks in the Outer Hebrides. On a clear day views from Clisham (799m) span from Cape Wrath to the Cuillins and St. Kilda. The glens are steep-sided with precipitous crags which, despite their relatively low altitude, give to the hills a mountainous character that compares favourably with better known mainland massifs. Exposure and grazing prevent tree growth, and the scenic quality depends on landform and intervisibility with surrounding landscapes, these doing much to enhance the significance of the mountains. In the east deep fjords, like Loch Seaforth, penetrate the hills, with the surprising presence of tidal water apparently far inland. The east coast of Harris is deeply dissected knock-and-lochan topography, with innumerable bays and islets, where the pattern of crofting settlement enjoys a particularly close relationship with the landform. It is a small scale landscape of detailed variety and visual pleasure that contrasts strongly with the softer, wider landscapes of the island's west coast.

The west coast is comprised of wide sandy machair-backed beaches, the bright clear colours of which lighten the dark greys and browns of inland hills and moors. These superb beaches are further enhanced by views across the vividly coloured inshore waters to islands and the North Harris mountains, which add not only visual interest but scale and enclosure. The rocky headlands that separate the bays have been sculptured by the ocean with geos and stacks. The scatter of islands in the Sound of Harris acts as a visual link between South Harris and North Uist, as well as creating a seascape of scenic beauty. The wide sandy strands of North Uist reflect much of the character of the west coast of South Harris, and similarly afford views across the sea to the mountains of North Harris. Loch Maddy and Loch Eport are indented sea lochs penetrating areas of low hummocky relief, containing much exposed rock and many fresh water lochans. Points within the area afford views north across the Sound of Harris, and only at the ridge of Marrival does this very diverse island scenery change.

OTHER NATIONAL INTERESTS

The Forestry Commission owns land near the head of Loch Seaforth, and the Department of Agriculture and Fisheries for Scotland owns land to the north of Lochmaddy, in South Harris at Uig and Langavat in Lewis. There are Sites of Special Scientific Interest at Glen Valtos, North Harris, Luskentyre, Northton, Loch an Duin, Loch Scadavay and Griminish.

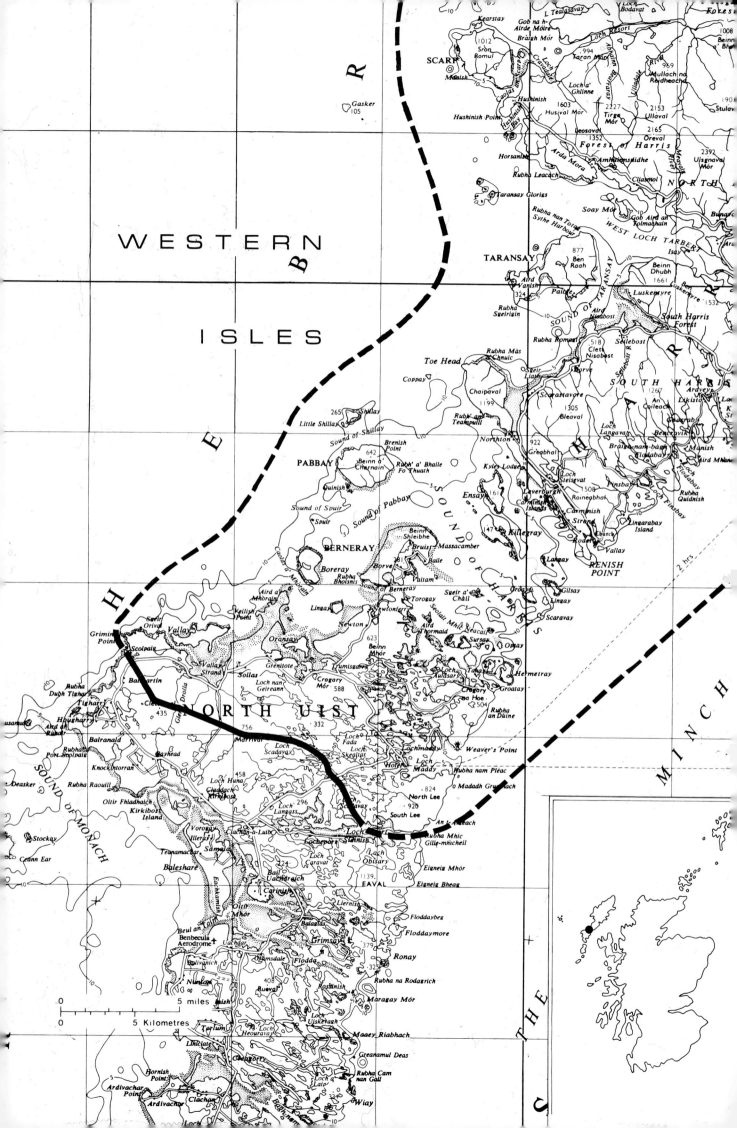

WESTERN ISLES ISLANDS AREA

900 HECTARES

ST. KILDA

EXTENT OF AREA

The area comprises the whole island group of St. Kilda, including Hirta, Soay, Boreray, Dun and the stacks of Stac an Armin, Stac Lee and Levenish.

DESCRIPTION

The description of St. Kilda which does not contain superlatives has not been written. Situated 41 miles west-north-west of Griminish, the islands are of volcanic origin and have been weathered by the ocean into profiles which never fail to impress all who set eyes upon them. The three larger islands are all in excess of 370m (1,200 feet) high and each exhibits precipices which plunge from that height into the sea. Stark, black, precipitous cliffs contrast with steep grassy green slopes and every element seems vertical. Caves and stacks are a feature of every coast except the smooth amphi-theatre of Village Bay on Hirta, and the cliffs are thronged with sea-birds, gannet and fulmar being more prolific here than anywhere else in Britain. Sir Julian Huxley called Stac Lee '. . . . the most majestic sea rock in existence' and Geikie has described Conachair as follows:

'Nowhere among the Inner Hebrides, not even on the south-western side of Rum, is there any such display of the capacity of the youngest granite to assume the most rugged and picturesque forms. It is hardly possible to exaggerate the variety of outline assumed by the rock. To one who boats underneath these cliffs the scene of ceaseless destruction which they present is vividly impressive.'

Boreray and Soay are no less impressive with their cliff-girt green turf pasture, and Dun has a highly crenellated profile.

OTHER NATIONAL INTERESTS

The group is owned by the National Trust for Scotland and leased to the Nature Conservancy Council as a National Nature Reserve.

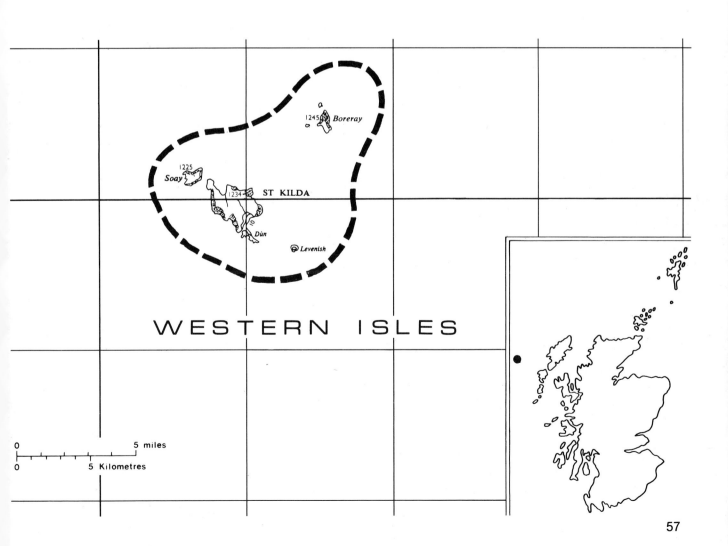

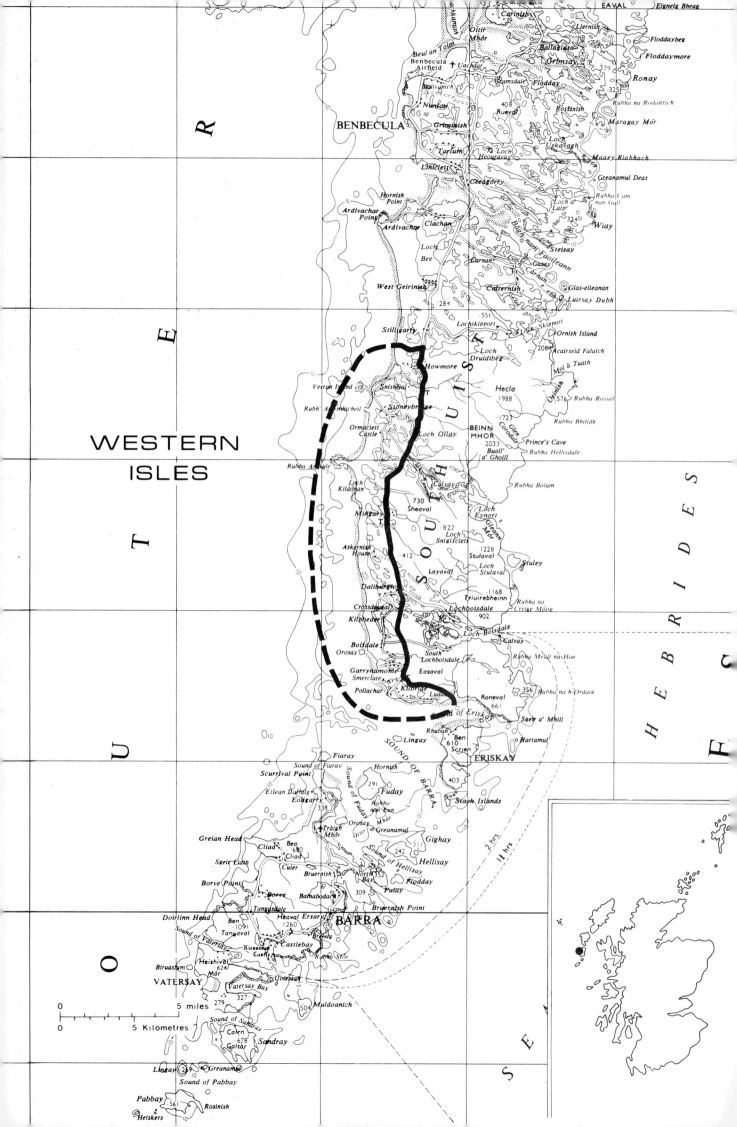

WESTERN ISLES
ISLANDS AREA

SOUTH UIST MACHAIR

6,100 HECTARES

EXTENT OF AREA

This area covers the machair coast of western South
Uist from Drimsdale, south of the rocket range, to the
southern extremity of the island. The western margin
is seaward, but inland the main public road B888
defines the eastern limit as far south as Loch Aisavat
at Smerclate, where the south face of Easaval as far
as Bagh Mor marks the limits of the area.

DESCRIPTION

The outstanding physical characteristics of the
machair are its low altitude and flatness, rarely
exceeding 30 feet in height. The land is interspersed
with shallow lime-rich lochans which make up about
one third of the surface area, and on the machair
itself between the lochans there is a pattern of
prosperous crofting settlement. This two miles wide
strip of lime-sand pastureland and water meadow is a
cultural landscape of strong individual character and
identity, not the least important element of which is
its flora. W. H. Murray has written (1973) 'Until a man
has seen a good machair . . . he may find it hard to
realise that . . . it grows not grass but flowers.
Amongst the most common are buttercup, red and
white clover, daisy, blue speedwell, dandelion,
eyebright, birdsfoot trefoil, hop trefoil, harebell, wild
thyme, yellow and blue pansy and silverweed.' From
May until August these flowers follow in seasonal
succession, but by August they have been cropped
by grazing so that green is the only surviving colour.
This succession of bloom, the dunes, the green
pasture, the pleasing pattern of settlement and the
beaches combine to form a landscape of great
character.

OTHER NATIONAL INTERESTS

A small part of the Loch Druidibeg National Nature
Reserve is included at the northern extremity of the
area, where the Howmore Estuary Site of Special
Scientific Interest also lies. Further SSSI are at
Rudha Ardvule and the Askernish Coast.

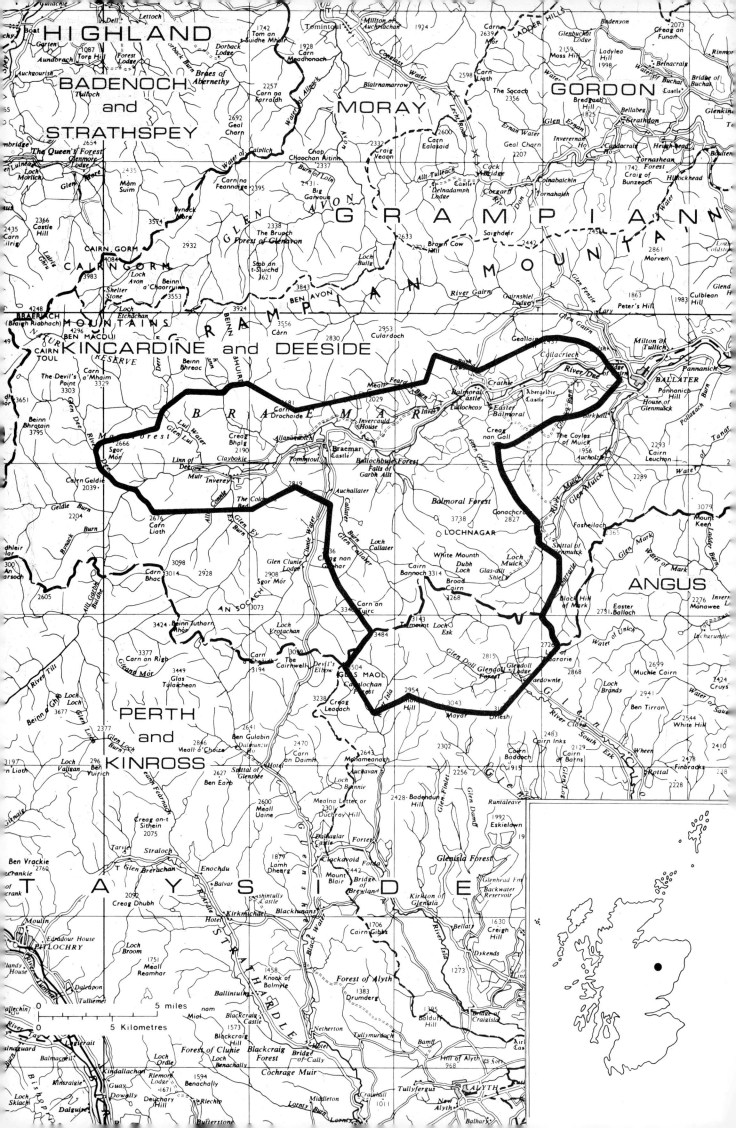

GRAMPIAN REGION

DEESIDE AND LOCHNAGAR

32,299 HECTARES — GRAMPIAN REGION
7,800 HECTARES — TAYSIDE REGION

EXTENT OF AREA

The area extends from White Bridge at Chest of Dee in the Mar Forest to the Knock, west of Ballater, and includes Ballochbuie Forest and the Lochnagar-Tolmount massif. The River Dee and Duncan Gray's Burn identify the western limit, and the southern limit is defined by a line connecting the salient summits of Carn Liath, Carn More (south of Inverey), Morven, Sron Dubh (above Auchallater), Creag nan Gabha, Cairn of Claise (1,064m), Glas Maol (1,068m), Sron Saobhaidhe, Finalty Hill, Mayar and Driesh (947m). The eastern limit approximates to a line through the summits of Lair of Aldararie, Ferrowie, Black Hill, An-t-sron (above Spittal of Glenmuick), Gonachraig, Creag nan Gall, Cairn Sgor-na-h-Iolaire, Creag Liath, to the Knock above Ballater. From the Knock the northern limits extend westwards to Glen Dee through the summits on the north side of the Dee: Geallaig Hill (661m), Leac Gorm, Meall Gorm, Creag a Chleirich, Carn na Drochaide, Meall an Lundain, Sgor Dubh and Sgor Mor.

DESCRIPTION

The character of Deeside is epitomised by the steep enclosing wooded valley sides, by continuous views of the river, and the unfolding of a new scene around each bend of the valley. Upstream of Braemar the valley has been widened and straightened by late glacial action. The Lui and Quoich waters enter the valley from narrow enclosed glens which afford walkers fine approaches to the Cairngorms. The flood-plain narrows at Linn of Dee where the river thunders through narrow rock-cuts and cauldrons. The valley floor has limited pastoral agriculture, and there are fine stretches of pine and birch woods with stands of Douglas Fir that reach up the side glens. Coniferous afforestation reinforces the natural woodland, and there is a planted admixture of broadleaved species in the many estate policies in the valley. The Ballochbuie Forest is a superb example of Caledonian Pine woodland, the beauty of which determined Queen Victoria to purchase the Lochnagar Estate to remove the threat of felling. The relationship of the fine woodland, with its understorey of heather and blaeberry, to the river and the flanks of Lochnagar form a significant landscape which has been further enhanced by the influences which Queen Victoria set in train. This is a very managed cultural landscape in which castles, large houses and their planted policies complement the natural character. It is this combination of intrinsic beauty and cultural elements which makes Royal Deeside famous.

Lochnagar (1,150m), Broad Cairn (998m) and Tolmount (958m) are significant summits in a mountain plateau, the edges of which have been sharply dissected by glacial erosion. It is a mountain core from which the deeply etched glens of Muick, Clova, Doll, Isla and Callater radiate, characterised at their heads by precipitous cliffs and crags. The summit of Lochnagar is further sculptured by huge corries containing lochans which in lesser degree are a feature of the whole massif, Glen Muick and Glen Callater also containing glacial lochs. The plateau is heather covered, '. . . . and nowhere else in the Scottish Highlands is there to be seen such extensive mass of purple bloom.' (Murray 1962).

OTHER NATIONAL INTERESTS

The Forestry Commission owns the Glendoll Forest and a small forest to the east of Invercauld. There are National Nature Reserves at Caenlochan Glen at the head of Glen Isla, and at Morrone Wood near Braemar. Sites of Special Scientific Interest occur at Eastern Cairngorms, Glen Ey Gorge, Ballochbuie Forest, Craig Leek, Crathie Wood, Lochnagar, Glen Callater and Coire Kander, and the Caenlochan Extension. The western extremity of the area includes a small part of the existing National Park Direction Area, and there is a Scottish Wildlife Trust Reserve at Glen Muick and Lochnagar.

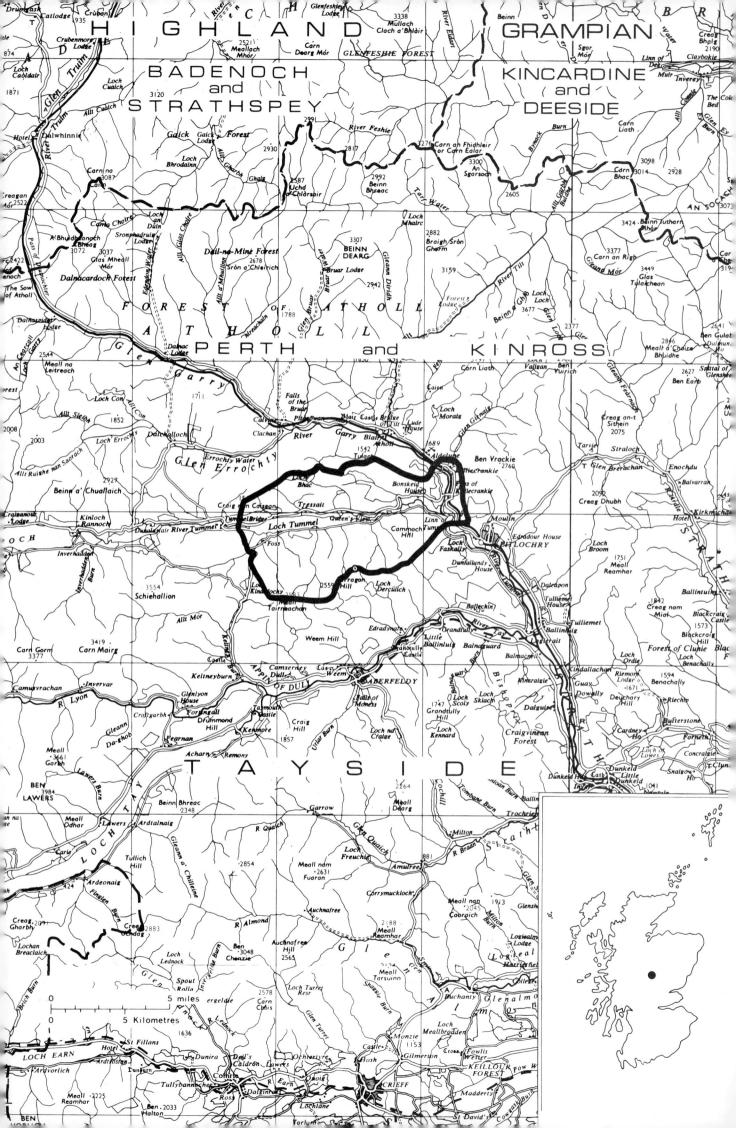

TAYSIDE REGION

LOCH TUMMEL

9,200 HECTARES

EXTENT OF AREA

The area includes the Pass of Killiecrankie, the northern reach of Loch Faskally and the Linn of Tummel, and Loch Tummel itself with the enclosing hills on both sides.

The western extremity of the area can be identified with a line joining the afforested Craig nan Caisean in Bohally Wood with the public road B846 west of Kynachan where it swings south to Daloist. From the public road the north western flank of Meall Tearneachain (780m) and the watershed eastwards through Farragon Hill (780m) to Wester Clunie define the southern limits. The summit of Craigower, and the other subsidiary summits of Ben Vrackie to the north above the Pass of Killiecrankie, form the eastern margin. The northern limits lie along the summit ridge enclosing Glen Fincastle as far as Meall na h-Imrich where the Forestry Commission boundary leads westward to Creag nan Caisean.

DESCRIPTION

The valley of the Tummel in the vicinity of its confluence with the Garry is very different from the stern straths of the north or the wild glens of the west. This is an upland sylvan landscape to which mountain peak, rocky crag, sparkling river and shining loch add a variety of incident. The deep gorge of the Garry in the Pass of Killiecrankie, with all its historical associations, the picturesque rapids of the Linn of Tummel, the bare overhanging heather-clad summits of the southern Grampians, and the prosperous looking houses and farms of the strath, are all framed in woodlands of an unusual richness and variety, the many species of which ensure constant but changing colour throughout the seasons. Despite the presence of main roads, railway, and hydro-electric installations, it is a landscape with sufficient strength of character for all the man-made intrusions to be dominated by the natural beauties of water, wood, and mountain. Westwards along Loch Tummel, notwithstanding the fame of the Queen's View, the topography becomes simpler and less intimate, but still displays a pleasing scene, composed of loch enclosed by wooded knolls and grassy braes, with fertile farms and estates, prosperous and well-populated.

OTHER NATIONAL INTERESTS

The National Trust for Scotland owns properties at Killiecrankie, Linn of Tummel and Craigower, and the Forestry Commission at Allean Forest, Faskally, and Tummel Forest. There are Sites of Special Scientific Interest at Tulach Hill and the Pass of Killiecrankie.

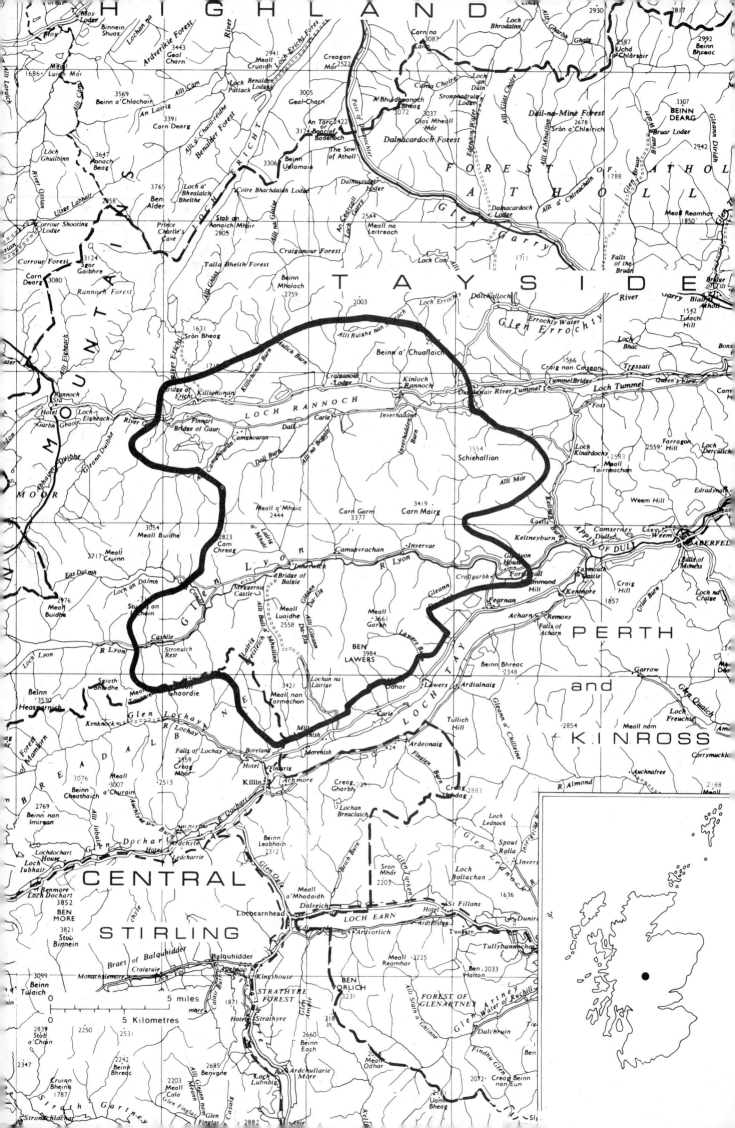

TAYSIDE REGION

47,100 HECTARES — TAYSIDE REGION
1,300 HECTARES — CENTRAL REGION

EXTENT OF AREA

The area includes Lochs Rannoch and Dunalastair, the peak of Schiehallion (1,083m), the Black Wood of Rannoch, much of Glen Lyon, Ben Lawers (1,214m) and Meall nan Tarmachan (1,043m).

The western margin runs from Sron Ruighe Clomhaiche above Bridge of Gaur, southwards to Meall Chomraidh, Meall Caol, Leagag and Cross Craigs. It continues south through the salient ridges of Cam Chreag, Creagan nan Gobhar, Coire Ban and An Grianan of Stuchd an Lochain to cross Glen Lyon at Dalchiorlich and reach the regional boundary at Meall Taurnie. The southern limits follow the regional boundary east along the watershed as far as the ridge of Beinn nan Oighreag and across the Lairig Breisleich to Beinn a'Bhuic, a western outlier of Meall nan Tarmachan. From there the limits flank the massif southwards to include the southern outlier of Meall Liath and swing eastwards to assume the southern boundary of the National Trust for Scotland property of Ben Lawers, to the point where it ascends the slopes of Meall Greigh. The easter-most ridge of the Ben Lawers massif is followed to a point above the public road from Fearnan to Duneaves where the limits cross Glen Lyon below Fortingall, to follow the Beinn Dearg and Meall nan Eun ridges of Carn Mairg to the Pheiginn Bothy and Dun Coillich. From Dun Coillich the Forestry Commission plantation boundary, and the Braes of Foss road define the eastern limits as far as Tullochroisk and the foot of Loch Dunalastair. The northern limit follows the first summit ridge north of Loch Rannoch back to Bridge of Gaur.

DESCRIPTION

The shores of Loch Rannoch, an open, spacious loch, are richly wooded. Pine, birch, oak, ash, larch, chestnut, holly, alder, cypress and juniper abound. On the south slopes of the loch is the great Black Wood of Rannoch, a remnant of the native pinewoods of Scotland. The north slopes are fringed with a more open canopy of birch woods which frame the views to be obtained from here of the almost perfect cone of Schiehallion, soaring skywards. Westwards along the broad loch are views of the distant hills of Rannoch and Glen Coe. The Loch of Dunalastair is a creation of hydro-electric works, but its reed beds and willow beds, and tranquil shallow waters, set amongst meadows and woodlands, offer a pleasing contrast with the bigger loch to the west.

Glen Lyon is separated from Rannoch by the broad summits of Carn Mairg. Said to be the longest glen in Scotland, it exhibits along its length a great diversity of glen scenery. Deeply entrenched between Carn Mairg, and Ben Lawers and Meall Ghaordie, (1,039m) it descends from bare wild mountains around Cashlie to Gallin and Meggernie where a change occurs. Here it becomes a broad

LOCH RANNOCH AND GLEN LYON

strath with Meggernie Castle set in the midst of woodlands, its park traversed by the broad leisurely loops of the River Lyon. The woodlands clothing the lower slopes of the mountains contrast well with the barer but colourful higher slopes, and as one descends the glen, the farmlands of the strath and the woodlands of the lower slopes become ever richer and more varied. At each turn of the road, a new scene of river, wood, mountain and meadow is revealed, until at the Pass of Lyon the river rushes through a tight rocky gorge closely screened by magnificent canopies of beech, to open finally on to the pleasant purlieus of Fortingall. W. H. Murray has written (1963): 'Glen Lyon has no counterpart in Scotland. Other glens . . . . show a similar change from desolate upper reaches to lower fertility . . . . Others possess some unique feature of gorge, or loch, or waterfall, or forest, not to be seen in Glen Lyon. But there is none that displays such varied loveliness of river and woodland scene, and maintains it unmarred throughout so great a length of changing landscape.'

OTHER NATIONAL INTERESTS

There are National Nature Reserves at Ben Lawers and Meall nan Tarmachan, and Black Wood of Rannoch is a Forest Nature Reserve. Sites of Special Scientific Interest occur at Loch Rannoch, Dunalastair Reservoir, Tempar Burn, Schiehallion, Carn Gorm and Meall Garbh, Meggernie Wood, and Meall Ghaordie. The Forestry Commission owns extensive forests at Rannoch and several smaller forests in Glen Lyon. Ben Lawers is a property of the National Trust for Scotland.

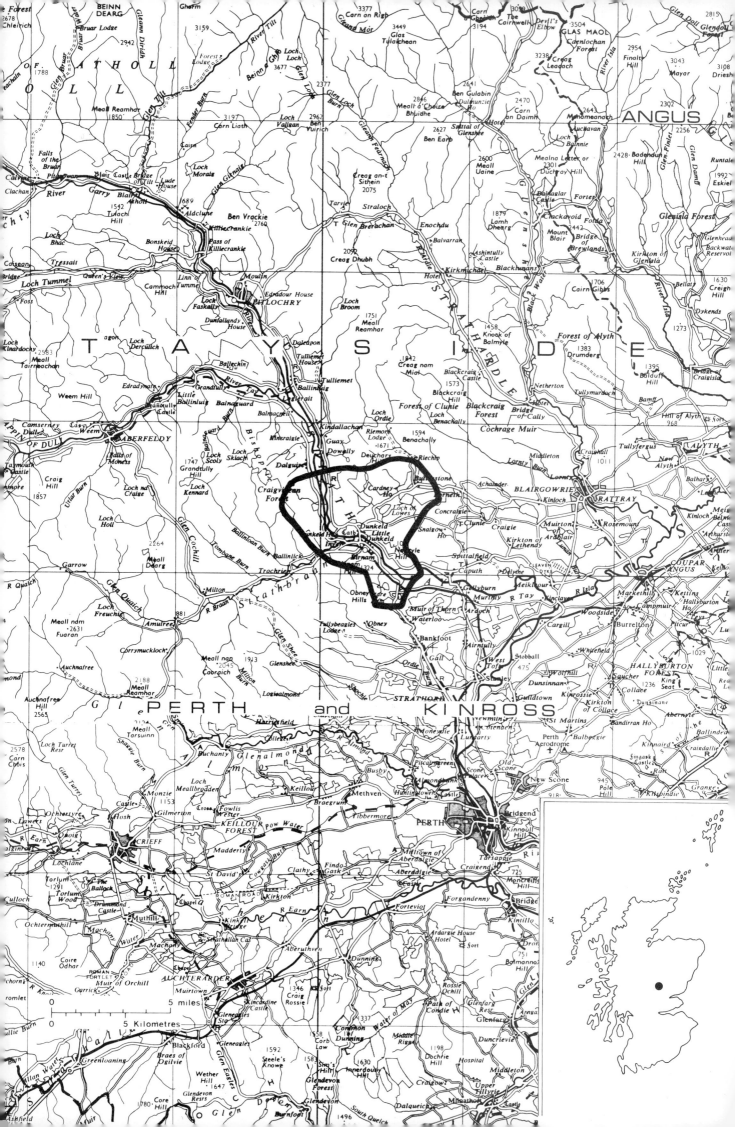

TAYSIDE REGION

RIVER TAY (DUNKELD)

5,600 HECTARES

EXTENT OF AREA

The area includes the zone of transition of the River Tay from highland to lowland river as it crosses the Highland Boundary Fault. On the west side, the Craigvinean forest boundary, from Creag Dubh southwards to Rumbling Bridge and on to the summit of Birnam Hill, defines the western extent of the area. The policies of Rohallion and the three 'dams' of Rohallion, Stare and Murthly Mill are included, and the eastern limit runs west of Murthly policies, Stenton, and Dungarthill, to Newtyle Hill. The parish boundary serves to identify the eastern limit from there as far as Laighwood, where it swings north to Arlich Hill, and then turns westwards through the summits of Coulan Hill, Knock of Findowie, and Rotmell Wood to cross the strath to Creag Dubh.

DESCRIPTION

The beauty of the Dunkeld area derives from the presence of the river between the rugged hills of the highland edge, which are clothed with a variety of different kinds of woodland, and the presence of a small and ancient ecclesiastical settlement. In addition to the Rivers Tay and Braan which contribute the interest of water to the scene, the former in great loops of deep shining peaty water, the latter in tumbling rapids and waterfalls, the area is peppered with lochans of varying size, many of which have been harnessed to human use and surrounded by broadleaved plantations. The northern part of the area consists of the broad strath of the Tay, strongly contained between heavily afforested valley sides where larch, pine and fir predominate. At Kings Seat, a narrow defile, the river swings east to flow between more broken hills clothed in oak woods and more mixed plantations. Below Inver where the Braan tumbles through the picturesque gorge of the Hermitage into the Tay, the haughlands are occupied by the little cathedral city of Dunkeld on the north, and the Victorian railway resort of Birnam on the south, then by pasture or woodland as the river winds eastwards out of the Highlands.

OTHER NATIONAL INTERESTS

The National Trust for Scotland owns properties at the Hermitage and in Dunkeld, and the Forestry Commission owns the Craigvinean Forest at Inver. There are Sites of Special Scientific Interest at the Lochs of Butterstone, Craiglush and Lowes, the last two forming a Scottish Wildlife Trust Reserve, and at Craig Wood. The southernmost island of the Shingle Islands Site of Special Scientific Interest is also within the Reserve.

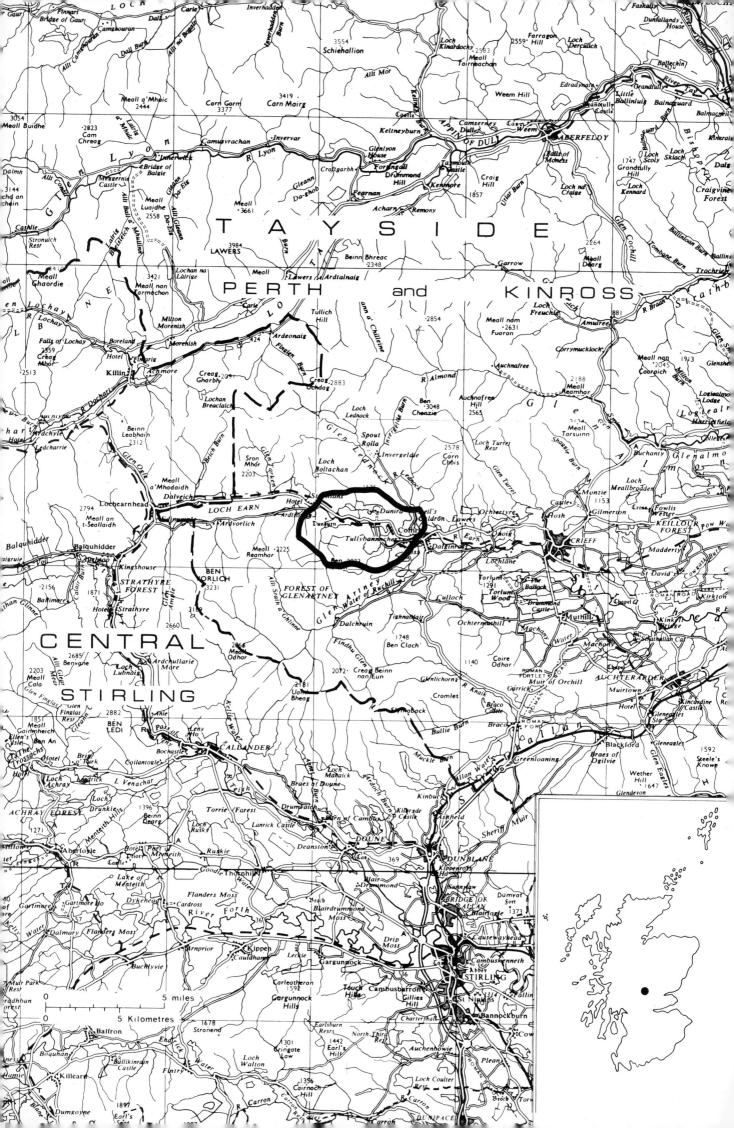

TAYSIDE REGION

RIVER EARN (COMRIE TO ST. FILLANS)

3,000 HECTARES

EXTENT OF AREA

The area includes the upper part of Strathearn between Comrie and St. Fillans, together with the peak of Mor Bheinn (640m). The western limit occurs at Little Port Hill and Am Bioran, and the southern limit is identified by Ben Halton and the public road from Ross to Cuilt, and the ridge above Comrie at the foot of Glen Lednock, including the gorge of the Lednock. Crappich Hill, Creag Liath and Little Port Hill define the northern extent of the area.

DESCRIPTION

This upper part of Strathearn lies at the conjunction of highland and lowland scenery, and the variety of landscape elements that derive from this combination result in a very distinctive character of pleasing appearance. There is a strong textured pattern resulting from the variety of vegetation and landform. The hillsides are punctuated by rocky outcrops and patterned with heather, bracken, grass or plantation. The valley has a strong sense of enclosure though the hills are not high. There is an intimacy of scale reinforced by the strong human influence of well managed farmland and woodland, but the hill tops have a wild rugged character. Plantations make a major contribution to the scene, the shape and extent of afforested areas respecting and relating well to the natural landform. There are very fine stands of broadleaved trees in the form of woodlands, parklands, and hedgerow plantings, and the river is alternately swift and leisurely, open-meadowed or alder-enclosed. Buildings are generally traditional in appearance and in tune with their surroundings. This is a landscape of great harmony.

OTHER NATIONAL INTERESTS

The Foresty Commission owns the St. Fillans Forest at Mor Bheinn, and Laggan Wood above Comrie. The Comrie Complex Site of Special Scientific Interest in Glen Lednock lies partly within the northeastern margin of the area.

69

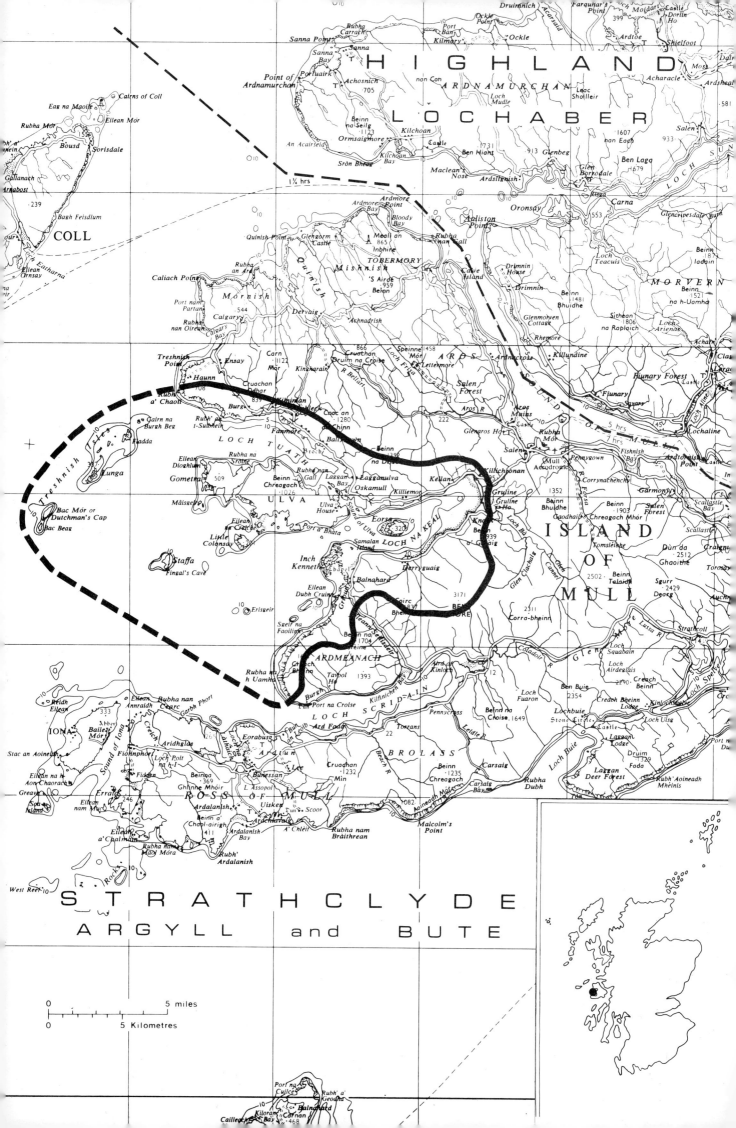

STRATHCLYDE REGION LOCH NA KEAL, ISLE OF MULL

12,700 HECTARES

EXTENT OF AREA

The area includes the sea lochs of Loch na Keal and
Loch Tuath, the islands of Eorsa, Inch Kenneth, Little
Colonsay, Ulva, Gometra and Staffa, and the
Treshnish Isles. On the seaward side the western
margin includes the Treshnish group, and extends
from Treshnish Point to Ardmeanach (Fionn
Aoineadh). Inland the eastern margin follows the
western salients of the Ardmeanach peninsula to
A'Mhaol Mhor (432m) and the Maol nan Damh and
A'Chioch ridges of Ben More (966m) to descend to
Knock. The public roads B8035 and B8973 as far as
Torr nam Fiann, and then the watershed between
Meall nan Gobhar and Cruachan Loch Trath
continue the inland margin northwards. From
Cruachan Loch Trath to Cruachan Treshnish the
limits adhere to the first salient summits inland.

DESCRIPTION

Loch na Keal is the principal sea loch on the Atlantic
shore of Mull. The outer loch is divided into two by
the island group of Ulva and Gometra, and the
northern water forms Loch Tuath. Although the
whole forms one island-studded seascape, the
component parts of Loch Tuath, inner Loch na Keal
and outer Loch na Keal have distinctive but
complementary characters.

The shoreline of the inner loch is of low relief, the
bayhead beach backed by meadow and woodland,
above which the south slopes sweep uniformly up to
the shapely peak of Ben More. Eorsa is a green
island of the same smooth appearance, but it is the
innermost of a group of islands in the outer loch of
astonishing variety of shape and form. The outer
loch has a bold and dynamic coastline of cliffs rising
in landslipped tiers, unmasked by tree growth, but
studded with huge boulders. The north shore has a
more intimate character which develops in Loch
Tuath where the shoreline is indented by a number of
small bays, into which hazel, rowan, and alder-lined
burns tumble swiftly and sometimes, like Eas Forss,
fall over small precipices which echo the larger cliffs
of the south shore. The hillsides of Loch Tuath have
a mixture of rough grazing and semi-natural
woodland which contributes to its more intimate and
gentle character. Although Loch Tuath has a sense
of enclosure that contrasts with the bold, rugged and
wild character of outer Loch na Keal, they share
views of the same groups of islands, whether the
dramatic profiles of the basaltic Staffa and Treshnish
Isles, or the greener, shelved islands of Ulva,
Gometra and Little Colonsay, or the innumerable
skerries that pepper the whole bight with
eyecatching shapes.

OTHER NATIONAL INTERESTS

The National Trust for Scotland owns the Burgh
estate in the Ardmeanach peninsula, part of which
lies in the area, and the Forestry Commission owns
woodland at Gruline which also lies within the area.
There are Sites of Special Scientific Interest at the
Treshnish Isles, Staffa, Gribun Shore and Crags,
Ardmeanach, Laggan Woods, An Gearna, and the
Central Complex of Mull at Ben More.

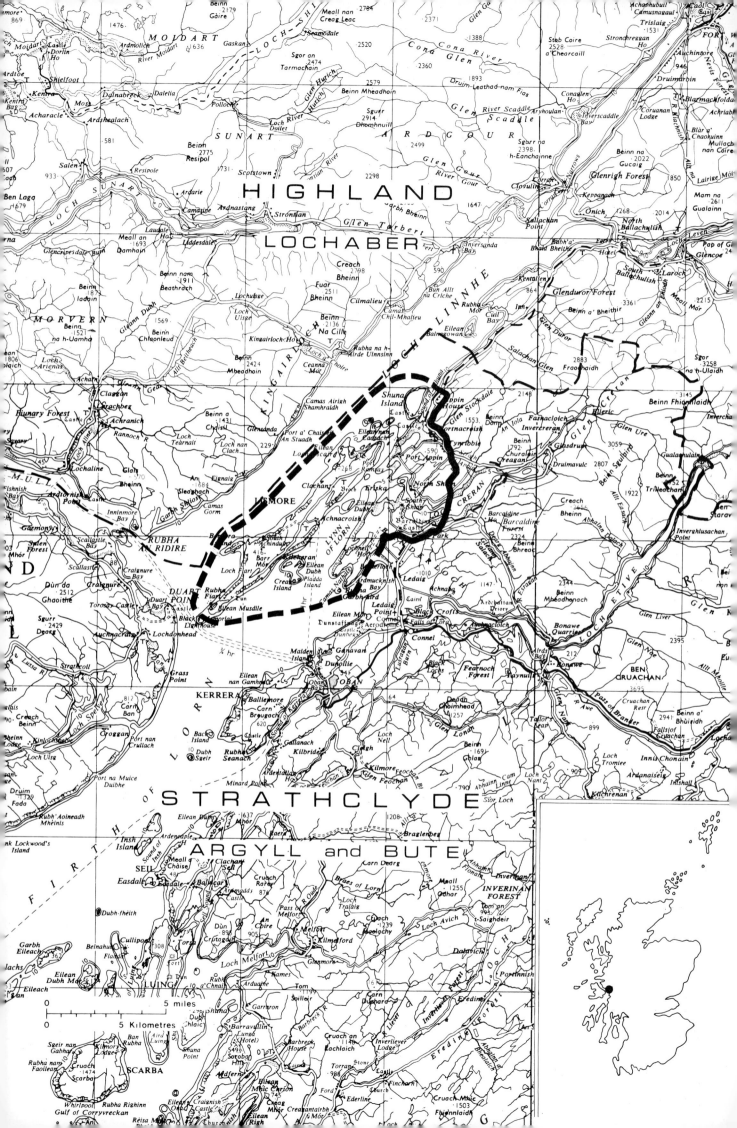

STRATHCLYDE REGION **LYNN OF LORN**

4,800 HECTARES

EXTENT OF AREA

The area includes the island of Lismore and its
attendant islets and skerries, Shuna, Appin, Eriska,
and part of Benderloch. The limits extend from Appin
House seawards around Shuna, Bernera and Eilean
Musdile to Ardmucknish Bay, and follow the water
course of the burn that drains Lochan Dubh, to the
main road opposite the entrance to Letterwalton
House. From there the main road is followed to the
headlands of Rubha Garbh in Loch Creran, and the
forest boundary to the road junction at Clarchasgaig.
From there the main road A828T defines the extent
of the area as far north as Appin House.

DESCRIPTION

The Lynn of Lorn is an island-studded waterway at
the confluence of the Sound of Mull with Loch Etive
and Loch Linnhe, from which it is separated by the
island of Lismore. The Lynn follows the
north-westerly alignment of the prevailing relief in the
area, which, set in the wider context of sea lochs and
mountains, is a small scale region of parallel
limestone ridges. It is these ridges, whether
submerged, so that only their tops form islets, or
whether raised in succession, with the waters of the
Lynn, Loch Creran and Loch Laich lapping in
between them, that give the area its distinctive
character. Made of limestone they support a rich
vegetation, either green, lush meadows in the
intervening glens and on the surrounding raised
beaches, or thick luxuriant oakwoods, at times
extended by new coniferous plantations, covering
their slopes. It is a small scale, secluded landscape,
with constantly changing views as the pattern of
ridges and valleys, islands and inlets, is traversed.
Lismore translates as 'Great Garden,' a name which
is not at variance with the character of the whole
area, and which is realised in the fine policies of the
big houses of the area — Lochnell, Eriska, Airds and
Appin, to which Castle Stalker on its diminutive
island offers a complete contrast.

OTHER NATIONAL INTERESTS

The Forestry Commission owns small tracts of land
at North Shian, Airds Hill and around Lochan Dubh.
There are Sites of Special Scientific Interest covering
the small islands in the Lynn of Lorn, the lochs on
Lismore, and Bernera Island. The area lies within the
existing National Park Direction Area of Ben Nevis,
Glen Coe and the Black Mount.

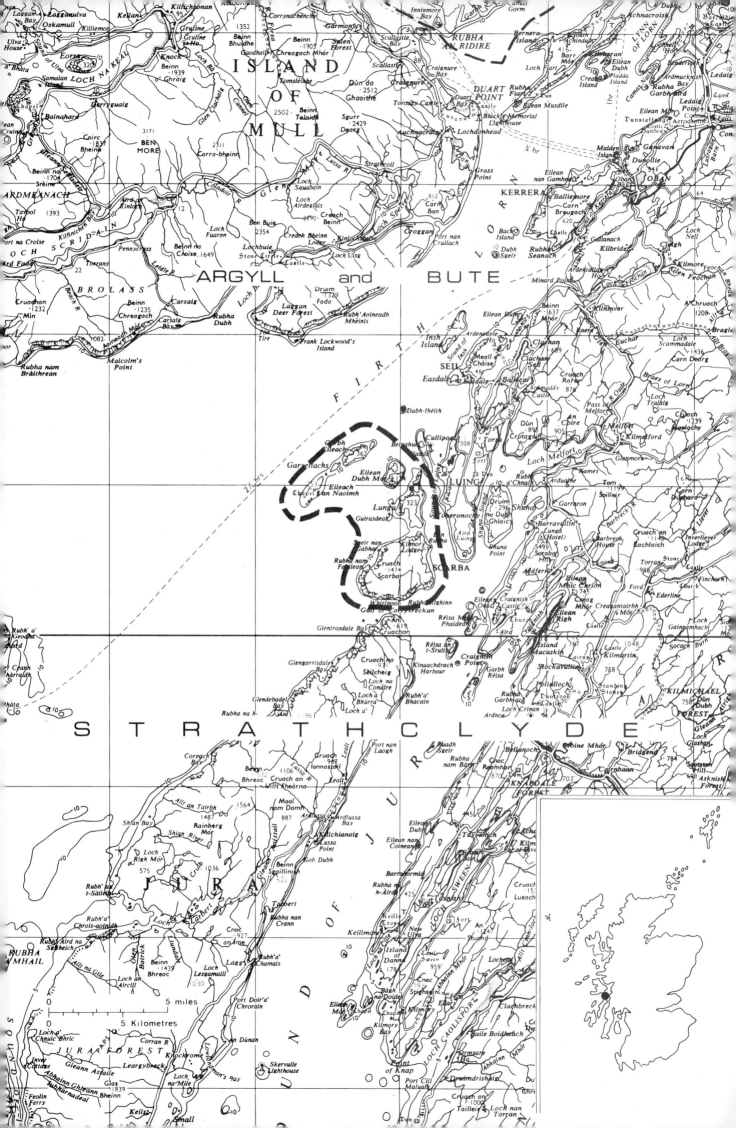

STRATHCLYDE REGION SCARBA, LUNGA AND THE GARVELLACHS

1,900 HECTARES

EXTENT OF AREA

The area includes the islands of Scarba, Guirasdeal, Lunga, the three Fiolas, Ormsa, Fladda and Belnahua, Eilean Dubh Beag and Mor, and the four islands of the Garvellach group, together with all their attendant skerries. This group of islands lies on the west side of the Sound of Luing which is the principal passage between Loch Linnhe and the Sound of Jura.

DESCRIPTION

In the clutter of islands in South West Argyll one group stands out in many views, and by virtue of its form, relief and inter-relationships makes up an area of varied character and distinctive identity. The holy 'Isles of the Sea' or 'Rough Islands' as the Garvellachs are otherwise called, are sharply angular when viewed from the north-east, and present vertical cliffs to the north-west. Inwards to the rest of the group, they are green scrub-clad islets, rich in flowers among the pink quartzose limestone boulders. They carry the most ancient ecclesiastical buildings in Scotland, and contrast strangely with the black slatey profiles of Belnahua and Lunga nearby, where the derelict slate quarries glisten in the sun or raise bleak black unnatural profiles to the storm. The dark pyramid of Scarba (449m) raises its summit high above these lower islands, supporting moorland that is in striking contrast to their green meadows or slatey wastes. On its eastern flank Scarba is well-wooded, an element of surprise in this oceanic context. Between the islands tidal races rip with a ferocity that is easily seen, and the streaming waters are themselves an important visual element in the total scene.

OTHER NATIONAL INTERESTS

The Garvellach Islands form a single Site of Special Scientific Interest.

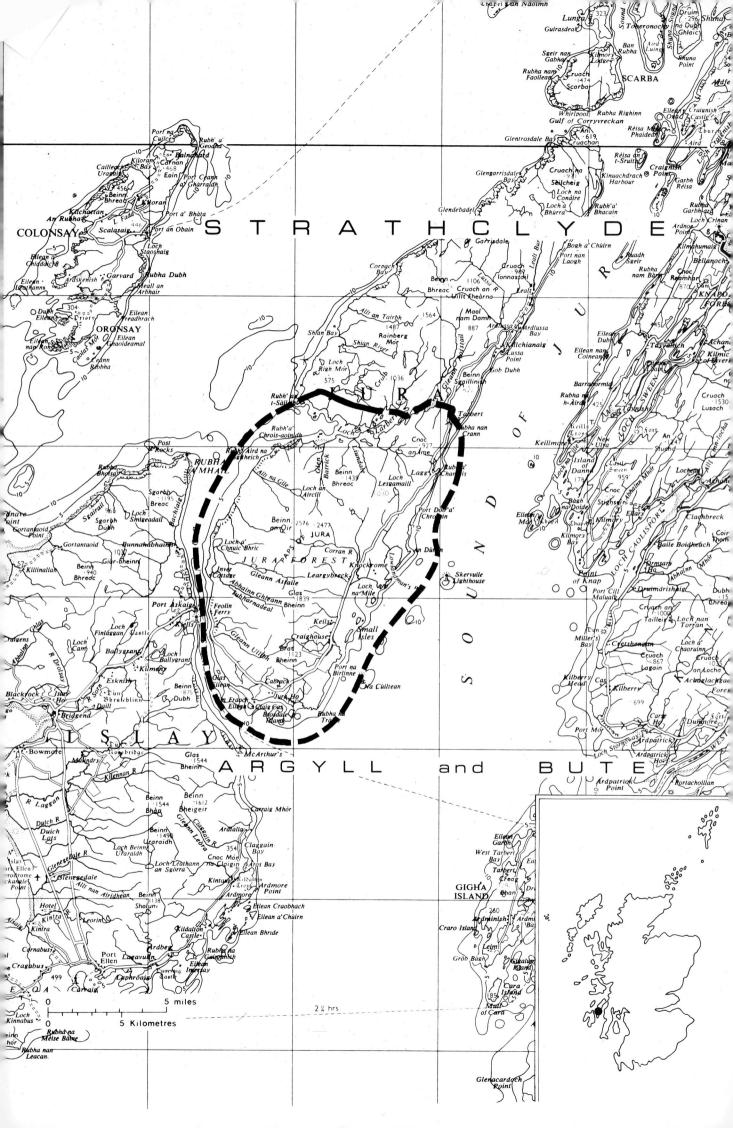

STRATHCLYDE REGION **JURA**

21,800 HECTARES

EXTENT OF AREA

The area includes the whole of the island south of
Loch Tarbert, and the immediate northern shore of
that loch up to the first summit ridges (Staon Bheinn,
Cruib, Glac Mhor).

DESCRIPTION

Jura forms the western visual limit of a large-scale
coastal tract which encompasses Mid Argyll, but it is
the southern part of the island which has outstanding
scenic interest. The island is made up of quartzite,
which usually results in remarkable upland landforms
and Jura is no exception. The Paps of Jura, all three
between 700 and 800 metres in height, are dominant
in views from the mainland and Islay. Their shapely
cones rise abruptly from rolling moorland, and their
summits shimmer with quartzite screes. 'In the
opinion of the well known Scottish writer Alisdair
Alpin McGregor, their steepsided elegance can be
compared only with the famous Cuillins of Skye'
(Whittow 1977). The coastal fringe has dramatic
raised beaches and cliff lines on the west side of the
island, and indented bays and islets on the east
shore, with some woodland, both semi-natural and
planted.

OTHER NATIONAL INTERESTS

The Forestry Commission has three small forests in
South Jura at Ardfin, Creag nan Sgarbh and west of
Craighouse, with a fourth holding at Lagg in the
north of the area. There are Sites of Special
Scientific Interest at the South Ebudes Raised
Beaches and at Craighouse Ravine.

STRATHCLYDE REGION **KNAPDALE**

19,800 HECTARES

EXTENT OF AREA

The area includes Loch Crinan and the Moine Mhor,
as well as the tightly folded ridge and glen
topography of north western Knapdale, around
Lochs Sween and Caolisport.

From Ben an Ardifuir on the north shore of Loch
Crinan the western margin runs down the Sound of
Jura past Eilean Mor and the Point of Knap to Port
Cill Maluaig on the south shore of Loch Caolisport.
The eastern margin is identified by the summits of
Cruach an Tailleir, An Goblach, Meall Ruadh, Cruach
Lusach, Cruach Breacain, Creag Ghlas, Cnoc na
Moine, the ridge behind Achnashellach and that to
the north west of Kilmichael Glassary as far as the
public road from the A816 road to Ballymeanach and
Poltalloch. This public road marks the northern
extent of the area. West of Poltalloch the summits of
Barr Mor and Ben an Ardifuir continue the northern
limit to the sea.

DESCRIPTION

The strongly grained topography of Knapdale, with
long parallel ridges and glens aligned on a
north-west south-east axis, presents a miniature
'Appalachian' type landscape. Heavily wooded now,
the glacially overdeepened glens either have narrow
ribbon lakes in their bottoms or else have been
invaded by the sea. Loch Sween is a complex series
of parallel channels intruding long narrow fingers of
sea into the coniferous forests of Knapdale. This ever
present combination of fresh and sea water with their
different plant life, small waterside meadows, and
heavily wooded ridges makes up a series of narrow
enclosed landscapes gradually opening out to the
lower, more open, and mixed land uses of the wider
topography at the mouth of Loch Sween, from where
there are fine views to the Paps of Jura. By contrast,
Loch Caolisport is a wide sea loch. It is contained by
sufficient amplitude of relief to frame the views of
Jura, and in this more open loch basin there is a
pleasing mixture of forestry and well kept farmland,
with moorland on the high land, and some deciduous
woodlands on the hillsides. To the north the flat
moss, meadow and arable land of the Moine Mhor,
the finely curving meanders of the River Add, and the
abruptly upstanding heights of Dunadd and Cnoc na
Moine, the former rocky and bare, the latter heavily
mantled in oakwoods, provide a sharp contrast to the
tightly grained and forested hills of Knapdale. Loch
Crinan, with its wide expanse of flats, continues this
character seawards, and is enclosed on its north side
by a series of miniature glens and hills, echoing the
scale of Knapdale to the south, but offering a gentle,
open, cultivated contrast to the forest. The historic
and cultural interest of this landscape adds a further
dimension to the scene.

OTHER NATIONAL INTERESTS

The Forestry Commission owns the considerable
woodland of Knapdale Forest, which lies in several
parcels throughout the area. There are Sites of
Special Scientific Interest at Ellary Woods, Danna
Island and the Ulva Lagoons, An Aird Tayvallich,
Taynish Woods, and Moine Mhor.

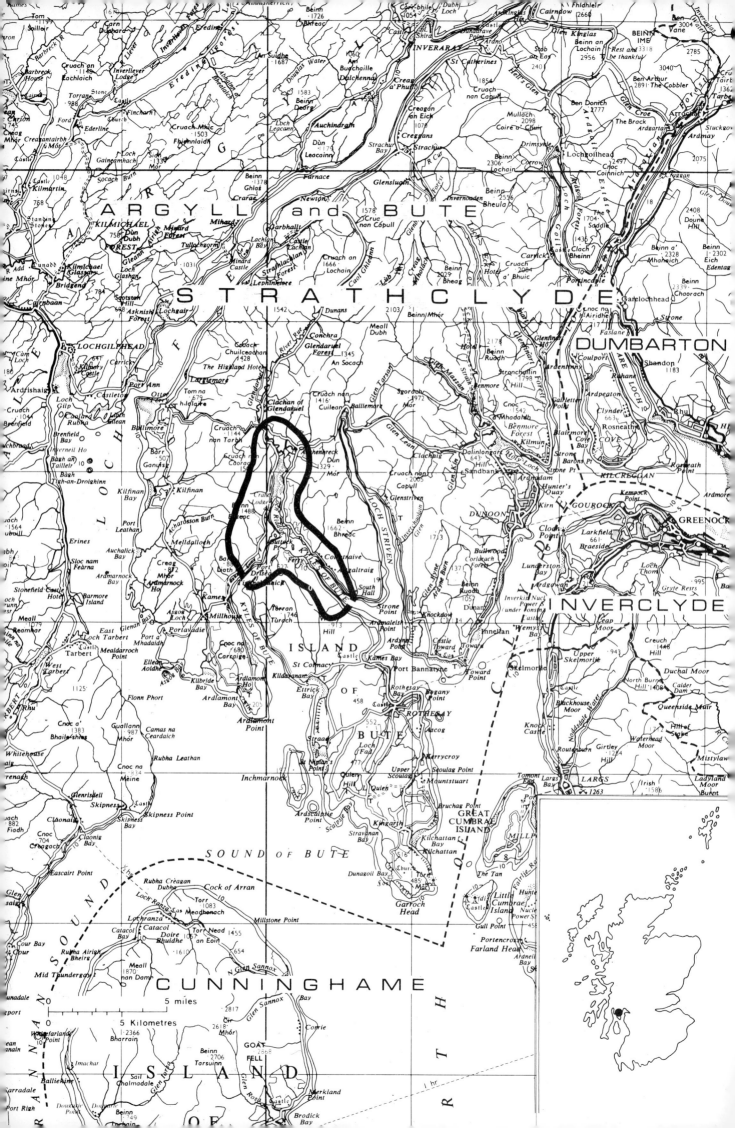

STRATHCLYDE REGION **KYLES OF BUTE**

4,400 HECTARES

EXTENT OF AREA

The area includes the lower part of Glendaruel, Loch
Ruel (or Riddon) and the inner Kyles of Bute between
Black Farland and Shalunt.
   From the bridge of the Ruel at Waulkmill the
western margin follows the first summit ridge west of
Loch Ruel through Beinn Bhreac and Beinn Capuill
(435m) to cross the western Kyle between
Tighnabruaich and Port Driseach to Rubha Dubh
and Barlia Hill on Bute. The summits of Muclich Hill,
North Hill of Bullochreg and Windy Hill define the
southern extent of the area. Across the eastern Kyle
the limit is identified by the ridge separating the Kyle
from Glen Neil up to Meallan Riabhach (484m),
Toman Dubh, A'Chruach, and the first summits
above Stronafian and Auchnagarran.

DESCRIPTION

The juxtaposition of the island of Bute to mainland
Cowal at the mouth of Loch Ruel gives rise to a
deeply enclosed passage of the sea through an area
of broken and well wooded hill country, the whole
combining to form a scene of great variety and
interest. Loch Ruel is markedly tidal with extensive
mud flats at its head. The lochshore is mantled with
mixed woodland and the hillsides are roughly
undulating with rock out-cropping frequently. There
are views to northern Bute, which has an
undeveloped moorland character, with bluffs
containing the Kyles. The mainland hills overhang
the Kyles steeply, and afford striking views over the
three arms of water. The rich verdure of the banks,
and the high degree of enclosure confer an
appearance of peaceful calm on these narrow
waters, which underlines their physical beauty.

OTHER NATIONAL INTERESTS

The Forestry Commission owns forests at Caladh
and Glendaruel. A Site of Special Scientific Interest
occurs at the Ruel Estuary in Loch Riddon.

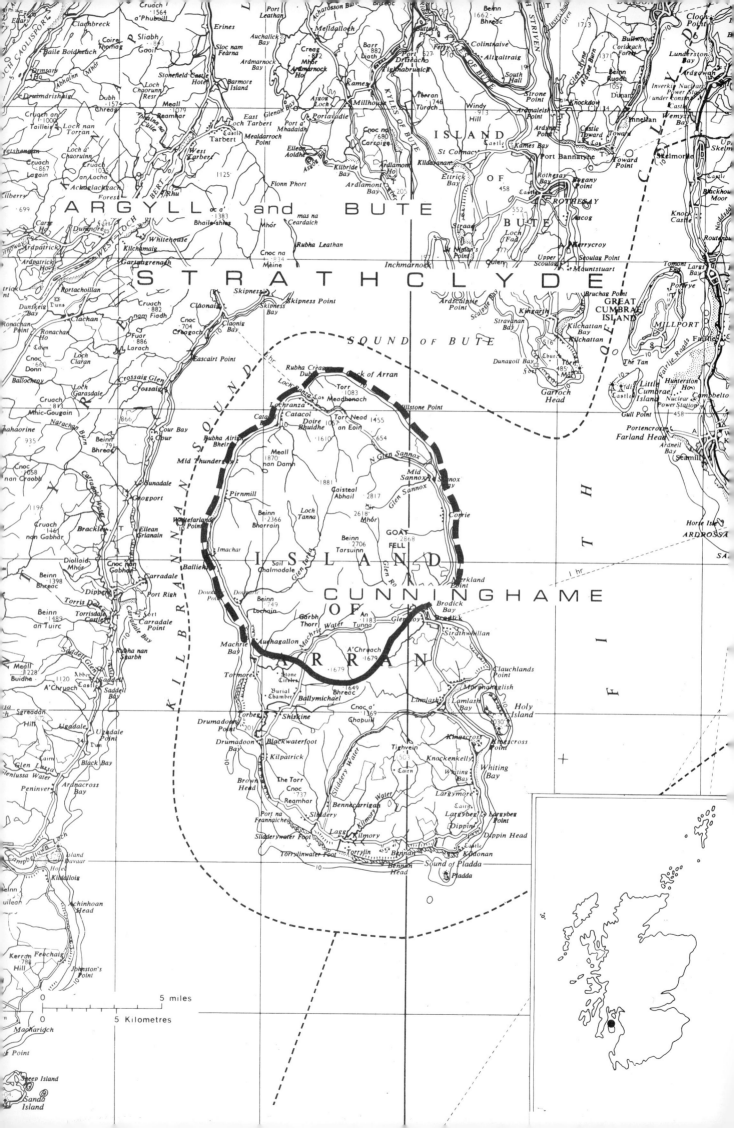

STRATHCLYDE REGION **NORTH ARRAN**

23,800 HECTARES

EXTENT OF AREA

The area includes the whole of the island north of a
line running from the mouth of the Glenrosa Water
westwards up the ridge of Muileann Gaoithe to the
summits of A'Chruach (512m), Beinn Bhreac (503m),
Ard Bheinn (512m) to the public road which passes
Machrie Farm and joins the A841 road at Cleiteadh
Buidhe.

DESCRIPTION

The Island of Arran makes a major contribution to
the wider landscape character of the Firth of Clyde,
its highland mountains being particularly
outstanding in a southern setting, and adding greatly
to scenic enjoyment of Bute, Ayrshire and Kintyre.
On the island itself, however, it is the northern part
which is scenically outstanding. Here the older
Highland rocks and a massive granite dome have
been fashioned into a deeply dissected highland
massif with rugged peaks rising to nearly 900 metres,
separated by deep glens. These mountains fill the
whole centre of the island and there is only a narrow
coastal plain before the boulder-strewn slopes
sweep upward to the shapely serrated peaks like
Goat Fell (874m) and Cir Mhor (798m). The coastline
has raised beaches on which typical clachan
settlements have developed, and where the mild
climate permits the growth of luxuriant vegetation,
best exemplified in the gardens of Brodick Castle
(National Trust for Scotland). If the island contributes
to all its neighbouring districts by its dramatic
presence, it must also be said that views from it to
Bute, Cowal and Kintyre also add to the quality of the
scene in Arran.

OTHER NATIONAL INTERESTS

The National Trust for Scotland owns the Brodick
Castle Estate, and the Forestry Commission has
several small tracts of forest at Merkland Wood,
North Sannox, Loch Ranza, Catacol Bay, Machrie
Burn, Cnoc na Ceillie and Glen Craigag. There is a
National Nature Reserve at Glen Diomhan and Sites
of Special Scientific Interest at North Newton Shore,
Corrie Foreshore, the Arran Northern Mountains
(Goat Fell etc), Gleann Dubh, and Ard Bheinn.

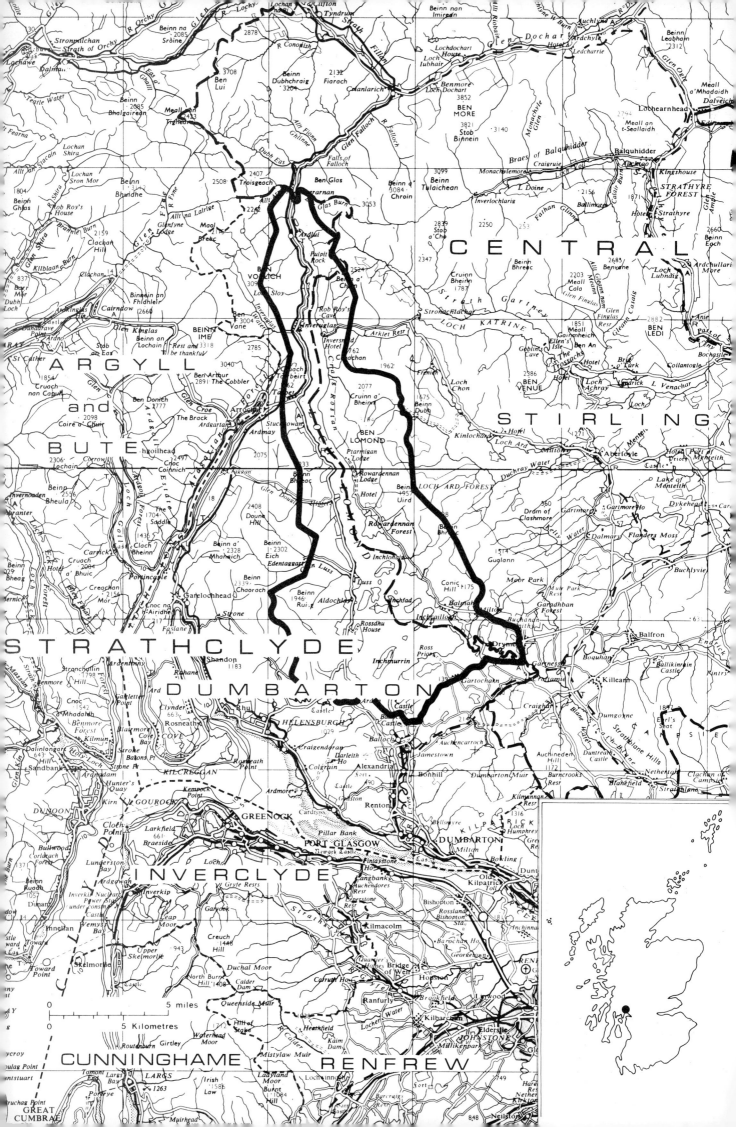

STRATHCLYDE REGION **LOCH LOMOND**

16,200 HECTARES — STRATHCLYDE REGION
11,200 HECTARES — CENTRAL REGION

EXTENT OF AREA

The area includes the immediate basin of the loch, but not all of its catchment, and Ben Lomond. The western margin is defined by a line joining the first summits west of the loch, commencing at Inverarnan and running via Garabal Hill, Ben Vorlich (943m), Cruach Tairbeirt, Ben Reach, Beinn Bhreac, Beinn Dubh, Coille-eughain Hill, and Balcnock (638m), whence the Luss parish boundary is followed to its conjunction with that of Kilmaronock parish to the south of Boturich. From Boturich, the southern limit of the area is identified by the public road A811 as far as Drymen Bridge and the entrance to Buchanan Castle. From here the farm access roads to Buchanan Home Farm identify the limits to the public road B837 which is followed westwards as far as Milton. The eastern limit follows the Burn of Mar to cut diagonally up Beinn Bhreac to its summit (586m) and then runs through Beinn Uird and Beinn a'Bhan to Glen Dubh and the Abhainn Gaoithe to the summit of Cruachan (537m). From here it continues northwards through Stob an Fhainne, Beinn a'Choin, Stob nan Eighrach, and Cruach to the Ben Glas Burn and Inverarnan.

DESCRIPTION

At the southern mainland extremity of the Highlands, Loch Lomond is the largest water body in Great Britain. The loch straddles the highland boundary fault, and thus has a variety of scenery stretching from the lowland character of the south shore to the deeply entrenched fjord-like northern head of the loch at Ardlui. There is a large amount of deciduous woodland, nowhere more noticeable than at the wide island-studded section of the loch, where the semi-natural woods of the islands are complemented by the fine policy woodlands on the shore. The east side of the loch also has extensive coniferous plantations which contribute variety to the scene as part of the Forestry Commission's Queen Elizabeth Forest Park. North of Ross Point the loch becomes a ribbon or finger lake, dominated by the towering summit of Ben Lomond (974m). Waterfalls, waterside meadows, and wooded promontories enliven the scene. The changing seasonal colours of bracken and heather, deciduous and coniferous woodlands, and the range of vertical relief, ensure that there is no time of year when the environs of the loch do not live up to their oft-sung fame.

OTHER NATIONAL INTERESTS

The Forestry Commission own the Garadhban and Rowardennan Forests, and the Queen Elizabeth Forest Park extends into the area. The Loch Lomond National Nature Reserve comprises Inchcailloch, the adjacent islands, and the Endrick Marshes, and the National Trust for Scotland own Bucinch and Ceardach islands. There are Sites of Special Scientific Interest at Inchmurrin, Inchmoan, Inchtavannach, Inchconnachan, and Inchlonaig, and at the Aber Bogs, Conic Hill-Arrochymore, Ben Lomond, Craigroyston (North and South) and Garrabal Hill.

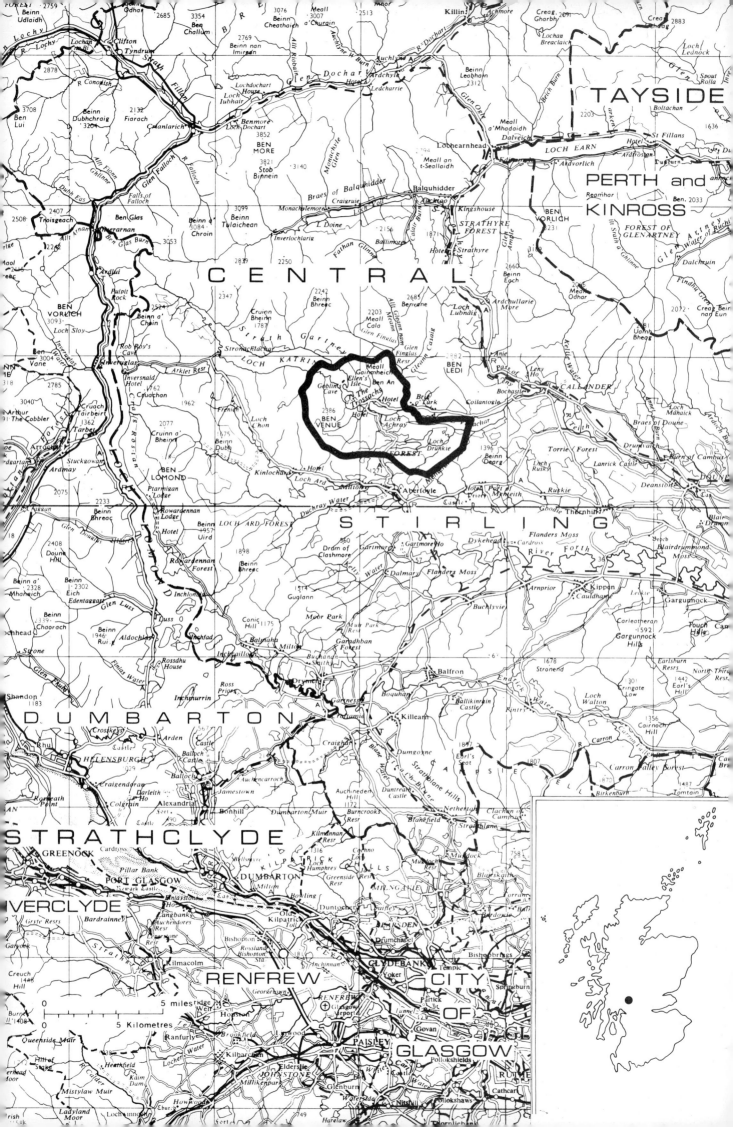

CENTRAL REGION   THE TROSSACHS

4,600 HECTARES

EXTENT OF AREA

The area extends from Ben Venue to the Menteith
Hills and centres upon Loch Achray and the east end
of Loch Katrine.

   The limits of the area run with the boundary of the
Queen Elizabeth Forest Park from Glen Finglas
reservoir to the vicinity of Lochan-nan-Ni, whence
they descend west-south-west to Glasahoile on the
south shore of Loch Katrine. The Allt Glasahoile
(eastern tributary) is followed to Creag Tharsuinn,
skirting the western flank of Ben Venue (730m)
where the Forest Park boundary is rejoined as far as
Creag Innich. From there the limits assume the ridge
over which the Duke's Pass crosses, and continue to
Meall Ear and the summit ridge of the Menteith Hills
which is followed to the shore of Loch Vennachar.
From that loch the eastern boundary of the Forest
Park is again followed, as far as Glen Finglas
reservoir.

DESCRIPTION

The highland scenery of the Trossachs is particularly
striking in comparison with the adjacent lowland.
The terrain is extremely broken and, although
coniferous plantations cover many hillsides, there is
a large amount of deciduous woodland, and
broadleaved trees fringe most of the roads, rivers
and lochs. A superb blend of mountain, wood and
loch, seen at its best in rocky Ben Venue,
overlooking the wooded shores of Loch Katrine with
its islands, bays and promontories, the area is one of
the most celebrated literary beauty spots in Britain,
associated with Scott and Ruskin. In 1974 Fiona
Leney wrote: 'Although the terrain is extremely
broken, the tree cover and quiet water bring a
gentleness to the rugged landscape. Compared with
the adjacent lowlands, the area is wild and rugged,
yet compared with the northern Highlands its small
scale and dense tree cover reduce its grandeur,
though contributing to variety and beauty. For many
people the scenery . . . . epitomises the landscape of
Scotland.'

OTHER NATIONAL INTERESTS

The Forestry Commission's Queen Elizabeth Forest
Park (Achray Forest) covers a large part of this area,
which also lies within the confines of the existing
National Park Direction Area. There is a Site of
Special Scientific Interest at Achray Forest.

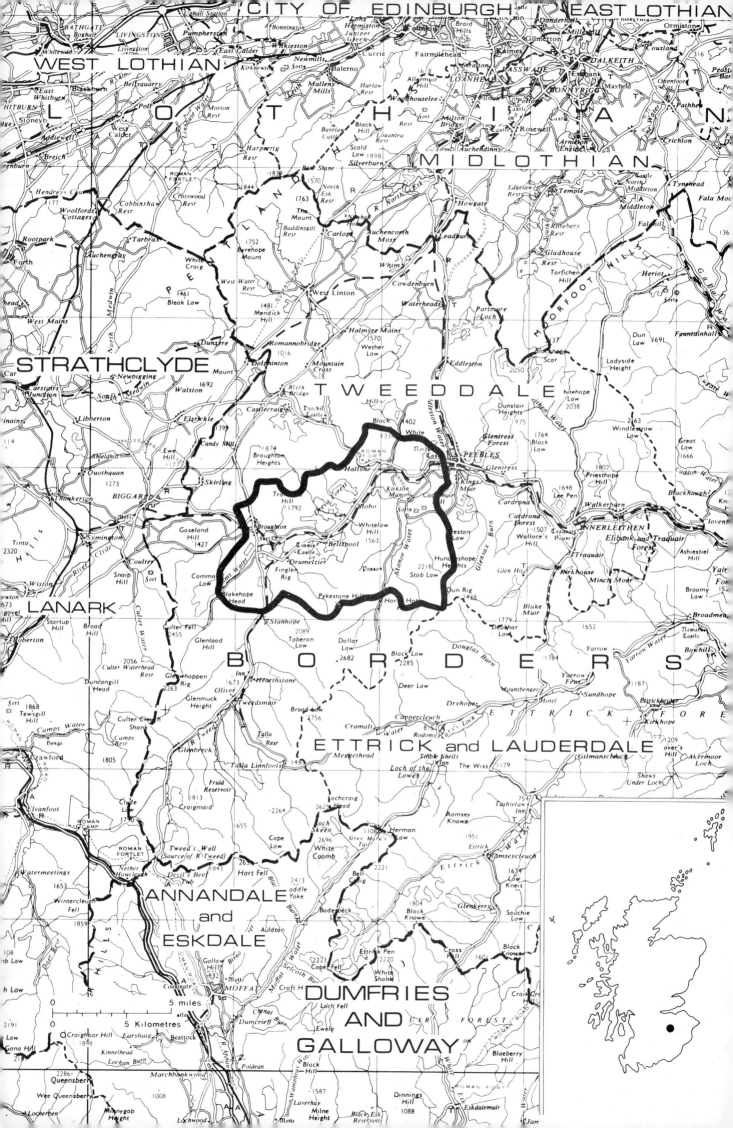

BORDERS REGION

UPPER TWEEDDALE

10,500 HECTARES

EXTENT OF AREA

The area covers that part of the Tweed Valley which
lies between Broughton and Peebles, together with
parts of the Manor and Holm Valleys and part of the
Broughton Heights.

   The western limit of the area extends from Clover
Law (493m) above Broughton around the west side
of the village to Whitslade Hill, Quarter Hill and
Blakehope Head. At Worm Hill (541m) the southern
limit runs across the main dale to Dulyard Brae and
Drumelzier Law (668m), Glenstivon Dod, Pykestone
Hill (737m) and Posso Craig. Here it crosses the
Manor Valley at Horse Hope Burn to Horse Hope Hill,
the Glenrath and Hundleshope Heights, descending
via Juniper Craigs to cross west of Crookston to
Cademuir Hill. From Manor Sware at the north end of
Cademuir the limits cross the Tweed again
immediately below Neidpath to swing west to South
Hill Head in the Meldon Hills, and on to Black Meldon
(468m). From there the summits of Hamildean Hill,
Torbank Hill, Penvalla, Hog Knowe and Hammer
Head return the northern limit to Clover Law.

DESCRIPTION

The upper course of the River Tweed is contained in
a narrow steepsided valley flanked by rounded hills
of considerable stature. The general sense of
containment created by the narrow valley is given
interest and variety by the inter-relationship of
woodlands, sometimes shelterbelt, hedgerow or
plantation, and both deciduous and coniferous, with
farmland which ranges from rough grazing on the
hill, through parkland, pasture and arable to riverside
meadows. The valley floor widens at each of the
confluences of the Holm, Lyne and Manor Waters to
give longer views into these tributary glens and the
higher summits at their heads, and then narrows
again at Neidpath where the castle guards the defile
between Cademuir and the Meldons. The river itself
contributes greatly to the scene, winding through its
haughlands with a majesty that assumes greater
magnitude than it really possesses. The dale is
ornamented with castles, mansions, kirks, and
prosperous farmhouses, and the hills marked with
the innumerable remains of ancient occupation.

OTHER NATIONAL INTERESTS

There are Forestry Commission woodlands at Glen
Holm, Rachan and Stobo. The River Tweed and its
tributaries constitute a Site of Special Scientific
Interest, and others occur at the Tomb Plantation,
Rachan, and at Stobo Slate Quarries.

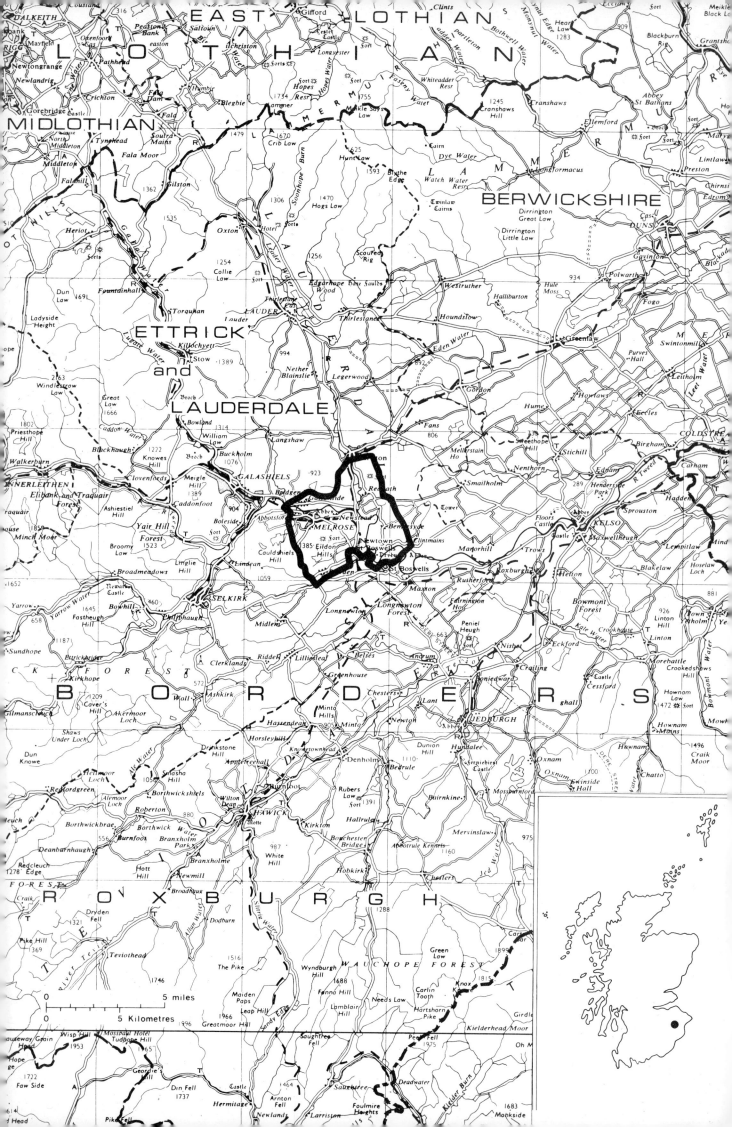

BORDERS REGION

EILDON AND LEADERFOOT

3,600 HECTARES

EXTENT OF AREA

The area covers the confluence of the Tweed and the
Leader, the Eildon Hills, Dryburgh, Bowden and
Melrose.

From Darnick Bridge over the Tweed, the western
margin is defined by the plantations of Huntlyburn
House'leading southwards to the public road B6359
at Bowdenmoor, which continues as the western limit
of the area as far south as the bridge over the
Bowden Burn, just before the crossroads of the
B6359 with the A699. The Bowden Burn identifies the
southern limit of the area which skirts Newton St.
Boswells on the west, north and east sides to take up
the line of the public road A6091 on the south side of
the town, as far as the northern side of St. Boswells.
The limits run between the village and the river to
cross the river at Norton Bridge. The eastern limits
run north-north-west from Clintmains along a series
of tracks leading to Redpath Hill, The Park, Black Hill
(314m), and White Hill which marks the northernmost
extent of the area. The northern limits of the area
follow the summits west and north of the Leader and
Tweed from Sorrowlessfield Mains to Camp Knowe,
Gattonside Mains and Darnick Bridge.

DESCRIPTION

Between its confluence with the Ettrick and that with
the Teviot, the Tweed exhibits neither the youthful
characteristics of an upland river, nor the mature
nature of a lowland river that it assumes below Kelso,
but its valley is wide and moderate, open and fertile,
while still affording fine views of the surrounding
hills. The scene comprises shapely uniform hills
enclosing the valley, the winding, incised and
wooded course of the river, mixed land use of arable,
pasture, plantation and moorland, and a settlement
pattern that still bears a scale and form closely
related to the topography. Adding drama to the
landscape the trio of the volcanic Eildon Hills
elegantly overhangs the valley, and dominates from
this position a wide area of Border scenery. Across
the Leader, Black Hill echoes their shape and
character, the whole area being seen to best
advantage from the famous Scott's View above
Dryburgh. Abbeys, bridges and mansion houses add
variety of incident to this very humanised and
cultivated landscape.

OTHER NATIONAL INTERESTS

The Department of the Environment cares for the
ecclesiastical Ancient Monuments of Melrose and
Dryburgh Abbeys, and the Rivers Tweed and Leader
are parts of the River Tweed Site of Special Scientific
Interest.

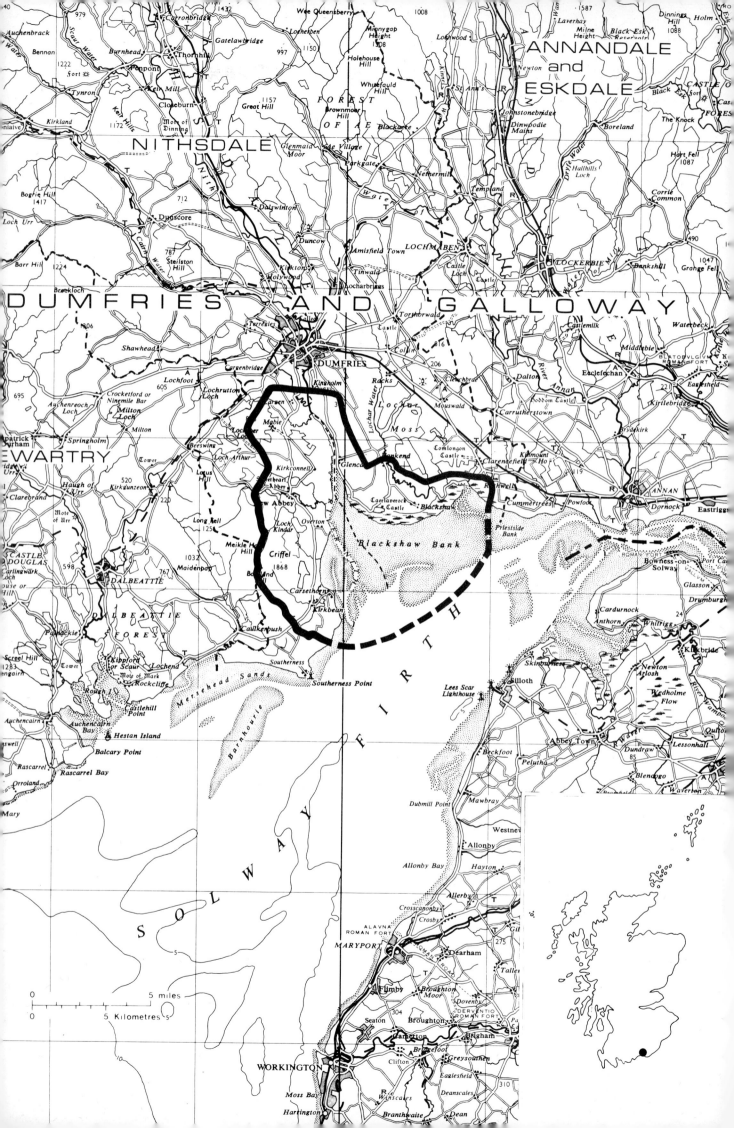

DUMFRIES & GALLOWAY REGION   NITH ESTUARY

9,300 HECTARES

EXTENT OF AREA

The area includes Criffell and Kirkconnel Flow, the
mouth of the River Nith south of Islesteps, Carse
Sands and Caerlaverock. The western limits are
defined south of Arbigland by the public road to
Powillimount from the main road at Newmains south
of the main road (A710), the ridge of Millour, leading
to Boreland Hill, the Glen Burn behind Criffell
(569m), and the western march of Shambellie Wood
continue the western limits northwards to the Mabie
Forest, where Marthrown Hill (249m), the mouth of
the Cargen Pow at Islesteps, and, across the Nith,
the track from Netherwood Mains to Netherwood
Bank define the northern extent of the area. From
Netherwood Bank southwards the ridge to
Chapelhill, and the public road B725 from Bankend
eastwards to the Thwaite Burn define the extent of
the remainder of the area.

DESCRIPTION

The River Nith and the Lochar Water flow into the
Solway Firth to form a wide tidal estuary comprising
the Carse Sands, Blackshaw Bank and Priestside
Bank. These extensive sands, mudflats, and saltings,
of an openness and horizontal scale unusual in
Scotland, are complemented and enhanced by the
presence of the gentle granite cone of Criffell and the
long well-wooded ridge extending back to
Marthrown Hill. The eastern flank of the hill, best
seen from Caerlaverock, has steep convex slopes
with a mixture of woodland and moorland
descending into the richer sylvan and pastoral
landscape around New Abbey. By contrast
Marthrown Hill is heavily wooded, but below it the
riverside flats are a mixture of pasture and peat moss
with associated birch trees. To the east of the tidal
channel of the Nith relief is low, but the long valley is
given emphasis by a long low ridge parallel with the
river. The river at this point is broad and bordered by
open fields, marshes and riverside trees in some
places. The variety of elements constitutes a whole
that is of great beauty, and constantly changes with
the coming and going of the tide, which in this
vicinity affects an intertidal zone of enormous width.

OTHER NATIONAL INTERESTS

There are National Nature Reserves at Caerlaverock
and Kirkconnel Flow, and Sites of Special Scientific
Interest at the Flooders, Kirkconnell Merse, and
Carse Bay.

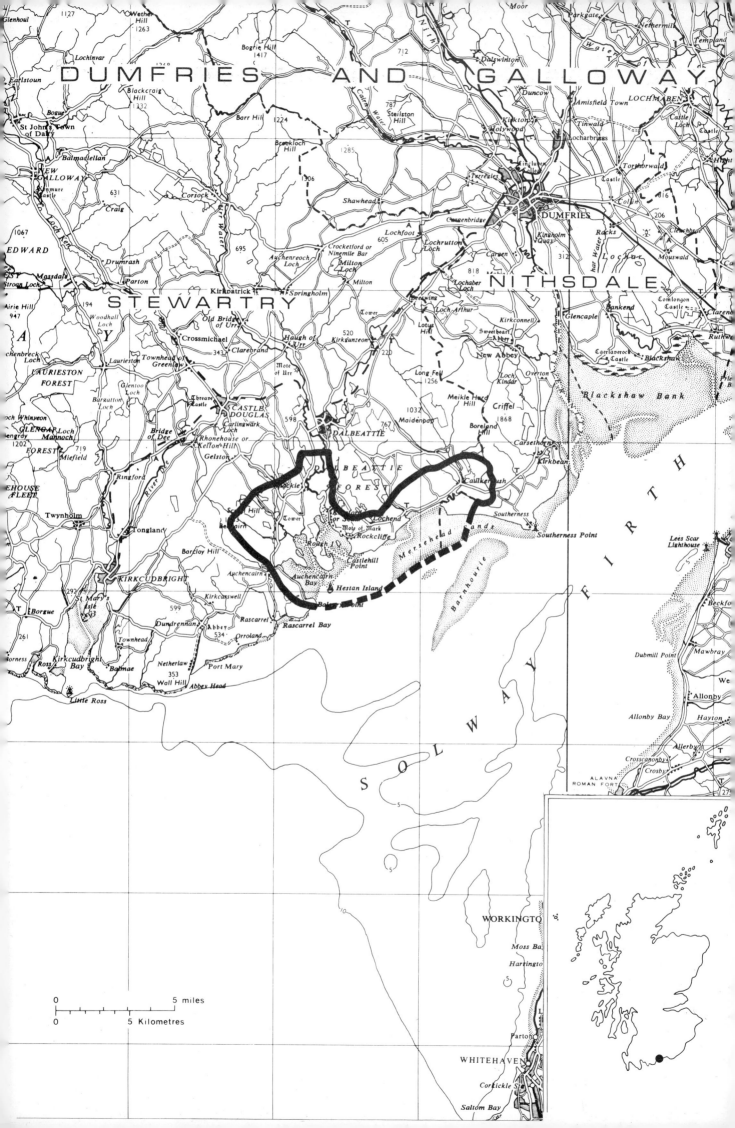

DUMFRIES & GALLOWAY EAST STEWARTRY COAST REGION

4,500 HECTARES

EXTENT OF AREA

The area comprises Auchencairn Bay, Orchardton Bay, Rough Firth, Sandyhills Bay, the Mersehead Sands and their immediate hinterlands. The western margin is defined by the ridge running from Balcarry Point to the summit of Bengairn Hill (391m). From there the inland limits run through the summits of Screel Hill, Croach Hill, Blackbellie Hills, Barlochan Hill and Ramshaw Wood to cross the floodplain of the Urr north of Munches to the main road A710. The main road defines the limit southwards as far as Woodside, and then the summit of the ridge of Mark Hill and Shiel Hill behind the villages of Kippford and Rockcliffe. From Shiel Hill the inland limits follow a line connecting with the summits of Barclay Hill, Bainloch Hill and Redbank Hill where they take up the line of the District boundary to Mersehead Plantation and the shore.

DESCRIPTION

The wide tidal flats of Mersehead Sands occur at a point where the saltings of Preston Merse meet the fossil cliffs and raised beaches of the rocky Sandyhills coast. Sandyhills Bay with its dunes and enclosing woodland is separated from Mersehead Sands by the meandering intertidal stretch of the Southwick Water which adds visual interest to the wide expanse of sand. Inland the containing hills are part wooded and part moorland, and at Caulkerbush there is a diverse pattern of hedgerow trees, parkland and wooded hillside. Westwards the hills become progressively more wooded in a way which strengthens the feeling of enclosure that they contribute to the inshore waters of Rough Firth, Orchardton Bay and Auchencairn Bay. Within the bays, divided by the wooded promontories of Almorness Point and Torr Point, lie Heston Island and Rough Island which strengthen the character of enclosed intimacy and shelter that these inlets exhibit. Around their shores the land use pattern of mixed farming and forestry and undulating relief underline this small scale intimacy of landscape, which contrasts well with the open character of the sand flats. The villages of Rockcliffe and Kippford add to the diversity of the scene, and elsewhere buildings tend to be of a traditional character which harmonises well with the nature of the landscape.

OTHER NATIONAL INTERESTS

The National Trust for Scotland owns Rough Island and land at Rockcliffe. The Forestry Commission owns scattered tracts of woodland at Kippford, South Glen, Auchencairn Moss, Dalbeattie Forest and Caulkerbush. There are Sites of Special Scientific Interest at Auchencairn Bay and the Southerness Coast.

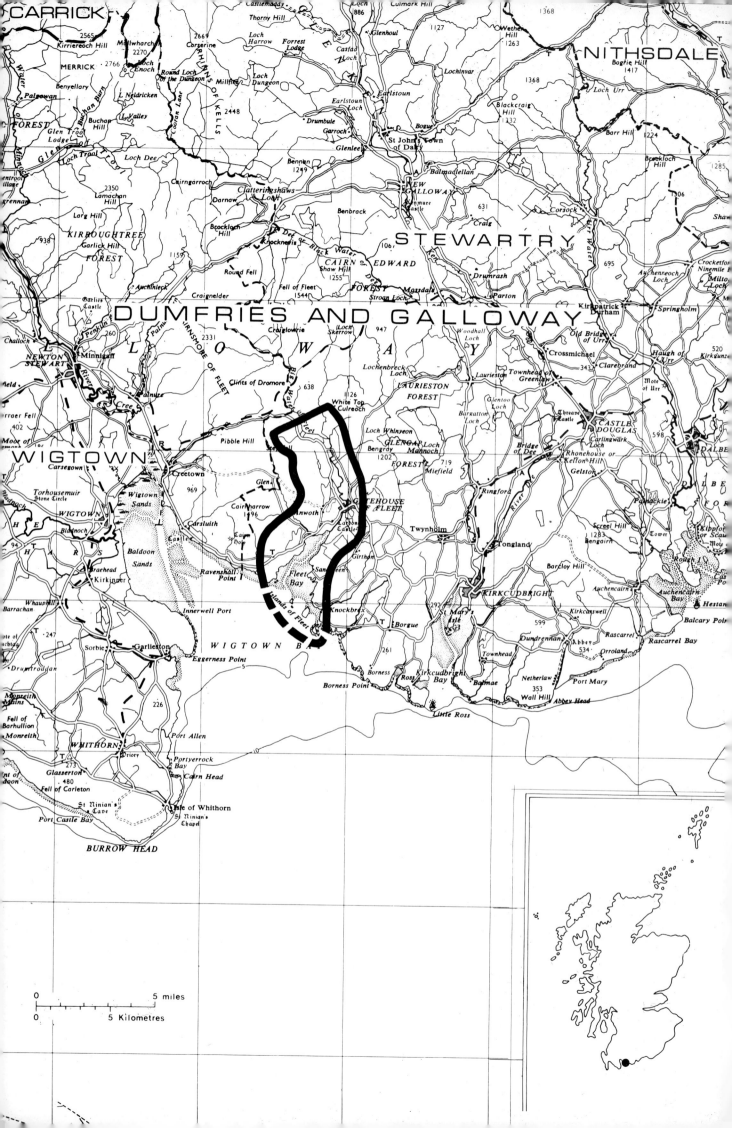

DUMFRIES & GALLOWAY FLEET VALLEY REGION

5,300 HECTARES

EXTENT OF AREA

The area includes Fleet Bay and the enclosing landforms on either side together with the valley of the Fleet inland as far as the southern end of Rig of Drumruck. The western limits run from Mossyard to Ben John, Mill Knock, Ardwall Hill, Kenlum Hill and Scar Hill to Meikle Bennan. The northern limits run from Meikle Bennan through Rig of Drumruck to Doon of Culreoch, and the eastern limits from Doon of Culreoch, via Castramont, Doon Hill and Bar of Barlay, to skirt Gatehouse of Fleet on the eastern side along the ridge joining Disdow Wood and Bar Hill. From Bar Hill the first inland ridge from Fleet Bay is followed to Barlocco Isle.

DESCRIPTION

Fleet Bay is dominated by the hill mass of Cairnharrow (456m) on its western side, of which Ben John and Mill Knock are outliers. On the east relief is not so pronounced but enclosure is given by the ridge which culminates in the well wooded Bar Hill just south of Gatehouse. Woodland contributes significantly to the Fleet Bay landscape, with policy planting and hedgerow trees being dominant. The village of Gatehouse of Fleet plays a prominent part in the scene, acting as a pleasing focal point for the valley which changes character at the village from estuarial to upland. While there is a greater amplitude of relief in the inner valley the landscape is also softer, more enclosed and intimate. There is a variety of woodlands from young plantations to mature broadleaved woods clothing the valley sides, while above them extends the open moorland of the hills, and below the riverside pasture. The pattern is one of rich, well-managed, mixed land use farming in which the woods are particularly striking, and where there is evidence of long established prosperity in the number of castles, churches, monuments and ancient remains.

OTHER NATIONAL INTERESTS

The Forestry Commission owns woodlands at Boreland Burn, Disdow Wood and in the Fleet Forest. There are Sites of Special Scientific Interest at Castramont Wood, Killiegowan Wood, and the Borgue Coast which extends as far as Fleet Bay.

BIBLIOGRAPHY

Berridge, N. G. 1969. A summary of the mineral resources of the "crofter counties" of Scotland. Institute of Geological Sciences. HMSO.

Birse, E. L. Assessment of climatic conditions in Scotland. The Macaulay Institute for Soil Research.
1. Based on accumulated temperature and potential water deficit. 1970.
2. Based on exposure and accumulated frost. 1970.
3. The bio-climatic sub-regions. 1971.

Blake, B. 1974. The Solway Firth. Robert Hale.

Brathay Exploration Group 1972. The Gairloch Conservation Unit, Wester Ross. A technique for monitoring recreational use in upland areas. Field Studies Report No. 19. Brathay Hall Trust, Ambleside, Westmorland.

Brown, Rosalind 1970. A roadside survey of Glen Coe. Unpublished report for CCS.

Burnett, J. H. (Ed.) 1964. The vegetation of Scotland. Oliver and Boyd.

Caird, J. B. and Moisley, H. A. 1964. The Outer Hebrides. In Steers, J. A. (Ed.) Field studies in the British Isles. Nelson.

Carmichael, Alastair 1974. Kintyre. David and Charles.

Countryside Commission for Scotland 1972. Torridon — conservation and economic opportunity. A case study. CCS.

Countryside Commission for Scotland 1974. A park system for Scotland. CCS.

Craig, G. Y. 1965. The geology of Scotland. Oliver and Boyd.

Crofts, R. and Mather, A. 1971. The beaches of Wester Ross. Department of Geography, University of Aberdeen.

Darling, F. F. 1947. Natural history in the Highlands and Islands. (New Naturalist) Collins.

Darling, F. F. (Ed.) 1955. West Highland survey. Oxford University Press.

Donaldson, J. C. and Coats, W. L. 1969. Revised version of Munro's (1891) Tables. Scottish Mountaineering Club.

Evans, F. J. 1972. The Trossachs report. CCS.

Feachem, R. 1963. Prehistoric Scotland. Batsford.

Geikie, A. 1901 (3rd Edit.). The scenery of Scotland. Macmillan.

Glen, Ann and Williams, Richard 1972. Scotland from the air. Heinemann.

Glasgow School of Art, Department of Planning 1967. Gairloch. Report for Scottish Tourist Board. Project No. 1.

Glasgow School of Art, Department of Planning 1970. Lochaber and North Argyll. Report for Scottish Tourist Board. Project.No. 2.

Great Britain: Command Papers, Government Reports etc.
Cmd 3851 1931. Report of the National Park Committee (Addison). HMSO.
Cmd 6631 1945. National Parks: a Scottish survey; report by the Scottish National Parks Survey Committee (Ramsay). HMSO.
Cmd 7121 1947. Report of the National Parks Committee (England and Wales) (Hobhouse). HMSO.
Cmd 7235 1947. National Parks and the Conservation of Nature in Scotland; report by the Scottish National Parks Committee and the Scottish Wild Life Conservation Committee. HMSO.
Cmd 7814 1948. Nature Reserves in Scotland; final report by the Scottish National Parks Committee and the Scottish Wild Life Conservation Committee. HMSO.
Department of the Environment 1974. Report of the National Park Policies Review Committee (Sandford). HMSO.
General Register Office, Edinburgh 1967. Place names and population in Scotland. HMSO.
Scottish Development Department 1967. Cairngorms area: report of the technical group of the Cairngorm area of the Eastern Highlands of Scotland. HMSO.
Scottish Development Department 1970. A strategy for South-west Scotland. HMSO.
Scottish Development Department 1972. The size and distribution of Scotland's population. HMSO.
Scottish Development Department 1974. North Sea oil and gas: coastal planning guidelines. HMSO.

Highlands and Islands Development Board 1974. Getting around the Highlands and Islands. HIDB.

Huxley, T. 1974. Wilderness. In Warren, A. and Goldsmith, F. B. (Eds) Conservation in Practice. Wiley.

International Union for the Conservation of Nature 1969. United Nations world list of National Parks and equivalent reserves. 10th Assembly of IUCN, New Delhi.

Johnstone, G. S. 1966 (3rd Edit.) British Regional Geology. The Grampian Highlands. Natural Environment Research Council. HMSO.

Kenworthy, J. B. 1972. The Wyllie-Fenton Field Centre, Bettyhill. Unpublished report, Department of Botany, University of Aberdeen.

King, C. M. 1966. Beaches and Coasts. (British Regional Geologies) Edward Arnold.

Leney, Fiona 1975. Landscape of Scotland. Unpublished report for CCS.

Landscape Research Group. Report of symposium — 3 May 1967. Methods of landscape analysis.

Land Use Consultants 1971. A planning classification of Scottish landscape resources. CCS.

Linton, D. L. 1968.   The assessment of scenery as a national resource. Scottish Geographical Magazine.

Loch Lomond Technical Group 1973.   A management plan for the conservation and controlled development of Loch Lomond.   First interim report, unpublished (for CCS).

McCormick, Donald 1974.   Islands of Scotland.   Osprey.

Mackenzie, O. 1921.   A hundred years in the Highlands.   Geoffrey Bles.

McLaren, M. 1973.   The Shell guide to Scotland.   Ebury Press.

McVean, D. N. and Ratcliffe, D. A. 1962.   Plant communities in the Scottish Highlands.   Nature Conservancy monographs No. 1.   HMSO.

Mather, A. 1969.   Glenstrathfarrar.   Land development survey.   Department of Geography, University of Aberdeen.   HIDB.

Miller, R. 1964.   The Geography of the Scottish Highlands.   In Steers, J. A. (Ed.) Field studies in the British Isles.   Nelson.

Millman, R. 1970.   Outdoor recreation in the Highland countryside. A study based on work for PhD thesis, Department of Geography, University of Aberdeen.   CCS and HIDB.

Murray, W. H. 1962.   Highland landscape: a survey.   NTS.

Murray, W. H. 1966.   The Hebrides.   Heinemann.

Murray, W. H. 1968.   The West Highlands of Scotland.   Collins.

Mykura, W. 1976.   Orkney and Shetland.   HMSO.

National Trust for Scotland, 1973 and 1974.   NTS yearbook.

Nature Conservancy Council, 1968.   Nature Conservancy Handbook, 1968.   HMSO.

Nethersole-Thompson, D. and Watson, A. 1974.   The Cairngorms.   Collins.

North of Scotland Hydro Electric Board, 1973.   Power from the glens.   NSHEB.

O'Dell, A. C. and Walton, K. 1962.   The Highlands and Islands of Scotland.   Nelson.

Phemister, J. 1960 (3rd Edit).   British Regional Geology.   Scotland: The Northern Highlands.   Natural Environment Research Council.   HMSO.

Richey, J. E. 1961 (3rd Edit).   British Regional Geology.   Scotland: The Tertiary Volcanic Districts.   Natural Envionment Research Council.   HMSO.

Scottish Countryside Activities Council 1970.   Report on wilderness.   Unpublished report for CCS.

Sillar, F. C. and Melyer, Ruth 1973.   Skye.   David and Charles.

Sissons, J. B. 1967.   The evolution of Scotland's scenery.   Oliver and Boyd.

Skinner, D. N. 1964.   Glen Coe and Rannoch Moor Area of Great Landscape Value.   Report for SDD.   HMSO.

Skinner, D. N. 1975.   The coast of Scotland.   HMSO.

Stamp, L. D. 1946.   Britain's structure and scenery.   Collins.

Steers, J. A. 1973.   The coastline of Scotland.   Cambridge University Press.

Steven, Campbell R. 1975.   The glens and straths of Scotland.   Robert Hale.

Stevens, H. M. and Carlisle, A. 1959.   The native pinewoods of Scotland.   Oliver and Boyd.

Swire, O. F. 1961.   Skye: the island and its legends.   Blackie.

Swire, O. F. 1963.   The highlands and their legends.   Oliver and Boyd.

Tivy, J. 1964.   The Scottish marchlands. In Steers, J. A. (Ed) Field studies in the British Isles.   Nelson.

Thompson, F. 1973.   Harris and Lewis.   David and Charles.

Thompson, F. 1974.   The Highlands and Islands.   Robert Hale.

Tourism and Recreation Research Unit, 1973.   Research Report No. 11.   TRIP Series No. 1, System description. TRRU, University of Edinburgh.

Tranter, N. 1977.   Argyll and Bute.   Hodder and Stoughton.

University of Aberdeen, Department of Geography, 1969.   Royal Grampian country.   Report for Scottish Tourist Board.

University of Aberdeen, Department of Geography, 1969-75.   The Beaches of the Highlands and Islands of Scotland — 13 Regional Surveys.   Reports for CCS.

University of Edinburgh, Department of Geography, 1970.   The impact of tourist development in Upper Speyside.   Report for Scottish Tourist Board.

University of Manchester, Robinson, D. G. (Ed.) 1970-75.   The landscape evaluation research project.

University of Strathclyde, Regional Studies Group, 1968.   The Galloway project.   Report for Scottish Tourist Board.

Wainwright, A.   Scottish Mountain Drawings:
  Vol I   The Northern Highlands 1974
  Vol II   The North West Highlands 1975
  Vol IV   The Central Highlands 1976.   Westmoreland Gazette.

Weir, T. 1974.   The Western Highlands.   Batsford.

Weir, T.   The Scottish lochs.   Constable.
  Vol I   1970,   Vol II   1972

Weir, T. 1976.   Scottish islands.   David and Charles.

Whittow, J. B. 1977.   Geology and scenery in Scotland.   Pelican Books.

Williamson, K. and Boyd, J. M. 1963.   A mosaic of islands.   Oliver and Boyd.